# Contents

# Acknowledgements

This project originated with the Criminal Law Working Party at the Law Faculty of Queen's University, Belfast. Valuable contributions in planning and methodology were made by Kevin Boyle, Gill Boehringer, Des Greer and Michael Knight in the early stages of the project. The work on the Magistrates Courts Survey was carried out by the following students of the Law Faculty at Queen's University and of the Social Administration Department at the New University of Ulster: David Carson, Kieran Duff, Robert Ellison, Gerrard Henry, Michael Lagan, Mary Lenegham, Helen McAlinden, Mary McCracken, Leslie McDonnell, Robert McKay, Jim McKeown, Martin O'Reilly, Martin Short and Barry Valentine. Financial assistance towards this work was given by the Legal Research Committee of the Law Faculty, Queen's University and the Cobden Trust. Data processing was carried out at the New University of Ulster. We should also like to acknowledge the cooperation and assistance of court officials at the magistrates courts covered in the survey and of the Clerk of the Peace to the Belfast City Commission.

# JUSTICE IN NORTHERN IRELAND

## a study in social confidence

cobden trust

by Tom Hadden
and Paddy Hillyard

# The Cobden Trust

*The Cobden Trust is a registered charity undertaking research into the causes of injustice. We believe that this cannot be achieved merely by examining the processes and possible abuses of the formal relations between the citizen and the state. It is also necessary to analyse the political context within which legal, administrative and legislative control is initiated and operated. In this survey of justice in Northern Ireland, we have examined legal procedures in relation to the political situation in the province with particular reference to public confidence in the impartiality and integrity of the judiciary.*

*This report will be of interest to lawyers and politicians in particular, but we hope that it will also give the general public throughout Great Britain some understanding of the causes of the present crisis in Northern Ireland.*

**Christine Jackson** – Research Officer

June, 1973.


ISBN 0 900137 03 7
Cobden Trust, 186 Kings Cross Road, London WC1X 9DE
Printed by the Russell Press Ltd., 45 Gamble Street, Nottingham. NG7 4ET. Tel. 74505.

## CHAPTER I

# Introduction

The existence of satisfactory channels for the expression and the redress of grievances is an essential element in a democratic system of government. The primary channel for this purpose is political. Ideally, grievances are raised on behalf of those affected or concerned by their parliamentary representative who will seek to have matters put right through direct political pressure on the government. In practice pressures of this kind can usually be more effectively marshalled through the press or through radio and television, but the principle is the same. In either case the effectiveness of such pressure is determined by a mixture of the merits of the case, the strength of public opinion on the issue and the government's own political commitments. There is no right to redress in politics. But in an open democratic system there is a fair chance of securing some measure of satisfaction.

Where political pressures prove insufficient, there is a second channel of redress through legal action. This is more limited. It applies only in respect of certain more fundamental grievances, and in particular the abuse of governmental power. In any case of arbitrary, biased or unlawful exercise of power or force contrary to the rule of law, there is a formal right to redress which can be pursued in the courts.

Public confidence in the existence and efficacy of these two channels of redress is essential to the smooth working of democracy. The absence of such confidence has been and arguably remains a major cause of the continuing troubles in Northern Ireland. On the political level the minority long considered the Unionist government to be totally unresponsive to any form of reasoned argument on matters which concerned the allocation of political power and patronage. And it appears to have lacked confidence in the legal system as an alternative means of redress. Similar lack of confidence is currently growing among certain elements in the majority community. Where lack of confidence of this kind is combined with deep seated and fundamental differences in political objectives, the temptation to resort to violence and terrorism is great, particularly when as in Ireland there is a lively tradition of para-military activity in both sections of the community.

To state the problem in these terms does not necessarily imply that adequate political and legal channels for the redress of grievances have in fact been lacking. Lack of confidence is a social phenomenon which may spring from relatively small causes and feed on itself. The adequacy of legal channels of redress, in particular, may not be properly tested as a result of a prior lack of confidence in the prospects of success. But the result in terms of the resort to direct action and the danger of the escalation of communal antagonisms is likely to be just as serious whether the lack of confidence is mistaken or justified.

**Judicial Confidence in Northern Ireland**

This study is an attempt to explain some aspects of the deteriorating situation in Northern Ireland in terms of a lack of confidence in the judicial system, and to assess how far that lack of confidence was and is justified. It is not always easy to isolate this issue from the wider question of the initial and continuing rejection of the state of Northern Ireland itself by some Republican elements in the Roman Catholic community. But since there is likely to be a continuing need to separate questions of ultimate political allegiance from those of immediate justice, the attempt is perhaps worth making. Any prospective settlement is almost certain to contain provisions guaranteeing the fundamental rights of all citizens regardless of religion or national allegiance.

It is clearly of crucial importance to the success of any such settlement that there should be widespread confidence in the efficacy of formal channels for redress.

In theory Northern Ireland has always been a non-sectarian state in which the basic democratic rights of all citizens have been constitutionally guaranteed. The Government of Ireland Act 1920 stated this explicitly in Section 5 which declared, among other things, any law void so far as it gives preference, privilege or advantage or imposes disability or disadvantage on account of religious belief.

The reality was otherwise. The proud promise of a 'Protestant parliament for a Protestant people' was effectively fulfilled through the continued stranglehold of the exclusively Protestant Unionist Party in the Stormont Parliament. The system of local government in its turn was so organised as to guarantee the dominance of the Unionists even in areas where they were outnumbered. The fundamental legal rights of all citizens were effectively annulled by the powers of arrest and detention granted to the executive under the Civil Authorities (Special Powers) Act of 1922 and 1933. This was initially introduced to deal with a temporary state of emergency, but has continued in force until the present. These powers were not formally directed against Roman Catholics and Republicans, but it was common knowledge that that was what they were meant for.

The Unionists sought in this way to secure themselves against ordinary political challenge and against external and internal terrorist attacks. There is little doubt that some at least of their practices were a direct or indirect infringement of the constitutional guarantees in the Government of Ireland Act, or of the common law. Yet there was no serious legal challenge to the Unionists prior to the development of the civil rights movement in 1968 and 1969. Since then there has been rather more emphasis on the protection of fundamental political rights by legal action. But the basic distrust of the legal system remains.

The explanation for this lack of confidence in legal channels for redress lies partly in the general lack of respect for all aspects of the Northern Ireland constitution among the leaders of the minority community. But a number of more specific allegations have typically been levelled against the legal system. These may conveniently be listed under three headings:

(i) the allegation that the judiciary in Northern Ireland has been almost exclusively drawn from committed Unionist supporters and may therefore be expected to refuse redress to a member of the minority community in any overtly political case:

(ii) the allegation that the Royal Ulster Constabulary, and more recently the British Army, have enforced the law in a partisan manner in any situation in which there have been political overtones:

(iii) that the Special Powers Act in particular has consistently been employed in a biased and partisan manner against the Roman Catholic and Republican community.

The rest of this study is an attempt to assess the validity of these allegations and their contribution to the general lack of confidence in legal channels of redress. In doing so we have explored a number of hypotheses. The first and most obvious possibility was that the allegations were true in whole or in part. The second was that while they were genuinely believed to be true, this was attributable principally to bias in the observer, either in the selection of material or the assessment of the evidence, or in the failure to pursue claims which could have been successfully pursued. A third possibility was that while the allegations might appear to be justified even to an unbiased observer, the true explanation of the apparent injustice was not deliberate or even unconscious sectarian discrimination but other social and economic factors: for instance, an apparent difference in the treatment of Roman Catholic and Protestant defendants might be due to discrimination in respect of social class in that both Protestant and Catholic defendants of a low social status may be treated in a discriminatory manner in comparison with defendants of higher social status. The final and perhaps most likely possibility was a combination of any or all of these.

Some of the material which we have drawn on in the analysis of these various possibilities in the chapters which follow is necessarily subjective and unquantified. We have made use of the findings of a small sample survey of the operation of magistrates' courts during the spring and summer of 1972, which was carried out by students of Queens University and the New University with the support of the Cobden Trust and the Legal Research Committee of Queen's University. We have also analysed the results of all cases heard at the Belfast City Commission between January and June 1973. The findings of these two studies have been incorporated into a general analysis of the operation of the legal system in Northern Ireland during a time of crisis.

## CHAPTER II

# Civil Rights
# The Failure of Law and of Lawyers

The present crisis in Northern Ireland arose directly out of the failure of a civil rights campaign. The term civil rights cannot be precisely defined and is increasingly used to cover the whole range of economic and political grievances. It centres on the assertion of a number of fundamental democratic claims for all citizens:

(i) the right to participate in the election of the government through a scrupulously fair electoral system;

(ii) the right to pursue legitimate political and social objectives individually or in association without interference from the government;

(iii) the right to share equitably in the allocation of state resources;

(iv) the right to rule under law rather than arbitrary or discriminatory acts of government.

These ideas may be expressed in simpler terms as the right of equal voting, the right of free speech and association, the right to a fair share of state resources, and the rule of law; they may also be expressed negatively as the right to freedom from gerrymandering, freedom from arbitrary arrest or censorship, and freedom from discrimination, whether in public housing, in public or private employment, or in the broader implementation of government schemes for social welfare and development.

The civil rights campaign in Northern Ireland, which seems to have developed in more or less direct response to the example set by the Blacks in the United States, was based on a denial of justice for the Roman Catholic community in all these respects. It is now generally accepted that the allegations were well founded. The Cameron Commission on Disturbances in Northern Ireland, set up in August 1969 in the immediate aftermath of the widespread rioting and disorders in Londonderry and Belfast and some other centres, listed among others the following items as major causative factors:

1. A rising sense of continuing injustice and grievance among large sections of the Catholic population in Northern Ireland, in particular in Londonderry and Dungannon, in respect of (i) inadequacy of housing provision by certain local authorities (ii) unfair methods of allocation of houses built and let by such authorities, in particular, refusals and omissions to adopt a 'points' system in determining priorities and making allocations (iii) misuse in certain cases of discretionary powers of allocation of houses in order to perpetuate Unionist control of the local authority.

2. Complaints, now well documented in fact, of discrimination in the making of local government appointments, at all levels but especially in senior posts, to the prejudice of non-Unionists and especially Catholic members of the community, in some Unionist controlled authorities.

3. Complaints, again well documented, in some cases of deliberate manipulation of local government electoral boundaries and in others a refusal to apply for their necessary extension, in order to achieve and maintain Unionist control of local authorities and so to deny to Catholics influence in local government proportionate to their numbers.[1]

To these might be added the specific complaint at the siting of most new economic development in the mainly Protestant area east of the River Bann and in particular, of the New University of Ulster at Coleraine rather than Londonderry. The Cameron Commission also mentioned the resentment among the Roman Catholic community at the continued existence of the Special Powers Act, and the exclusively Protestant 'B Specials', a paramilitary police force, both of which were designed and used to protect the Unionist state from Republicanism, whether by internal subversion or external attack.

The Cameron Commission concentrated its attention on the frustration within the Roman Catholic community at the failure of all attempts to use political channels to induce the Government to investigate and remedy these grievances. This was understandable since it was through political channels that the civil rights campaign had been pursued. But the failure of the civil rights leaders to make any serious attempt to obtain a legal remedy for their claims also requires some explanation. It is a primary task of law and lawyers to deal with basic grievances of this kind before recourse is made to direct action, with all the risks of riot and disorder which that may bring in its train. Why was it that in Northern Ireland this essential safety valve of legal redress was not there to avert the confrontation which so tragically developed?

**The Failure of the Civil Rights Campaign to Obtain a Legal Remedy**

The most obvious explanation for this failure of law and lawyers is the absence of any formal guarantees in the British and Northern Irish constitution of basic civil rights and the consequent lack of any tradition of civil rights litigation. This is in direct contrast to the situation in the United States and in the Republic of Ireland where such formal guarantees are included in written constitutions and have been relied on in court actions. The part played by the United States Supreme Court in the development of civil rights is well known. Some militant Black leaders and white observers have admittedly laid emphasis on the dangerous effects of Supreme Court judgments in raising expectations which could not in the event be satisfied by purely legal means, but the US example has shown the value of fundamental legal and constitutional guarantees.

The difference in legal tradition, however, is not a sufficient explanation of the course of events in Northern Ireland. The absence of formal constitutional guarantees in the British constitution does not mean that abuses of the kind alleged in Northern Ireland could not have been remedied at law. The use of statutory powers in bad faith or for an improper purpose is an established ground of legal challenge in English law. It seems likely that this objection could have been raised in respect of the more blatant instances of electoral gerrymandering with a genuine prospect of success, at least in those areas where local wards were so drawn that a substantial majority of Catholics were continually outvoted in local elections by a minority of Unionists. Furthermore, the specific constitutional guarantees against discriminatory legislation in the Government of Ireland Act could well have formed the basis of a challenge to the validity of discriminatory administrative decisions made under Northern Ireland Statutes, for instance in the field of housing allocation, as well as to the statutes themselves. This possibility is clearly stated in the leading text book on constitutional law.[2]

Nor can the failure to pursue the civil rights campaign in the courts in preference to the streets, be attributed to a lack of organisation or finance. At the party political level there was a lack of effective organisation and expertise among Nationalist and Republican representatives. There was no central party organisation or national conference until 1966. Candidates for elections were selected by *ad hoc* meetings of local notables, and after election pursued their own individual strategies and policies. But the Campaign for Social Justice, a highly professional and committed propaganda and action group centred in Dungannon, had been in existence since 1963 and from around 1966 there was a much greater degree of organisation and co-ordination among opposition M.P.s throughout Northern Ireland. There can be little doubt that these forces would have had little difficulty in raising the necessary funds and backing for a serious legal challenge to the various discriminatory practices maintained by local Unionist councils had they been convinced of the prospects of making any progress.

The necessary confidence in the judicial system as a means of securing justice, however, appears to have been lacking. It is difficult to produce firm evidence on matters of this kind other than the failure of civil rights leaders to initiate any legal action prior to the Republican Clubs case in 1968, and the Dungannon housing litigation in 1970/71. The attitude of the Campaign for Social Justice, which was perhaps the most likely sponsor of action in this field, is significant. The committee had assembled a sufficiently impressive dossier of discrimination in 1963 to make a direct approach to the British Prime Minister, Sir Alec Douglas-Home. Sir Alec responded by recommending legal action in the courts, though he also applied secret pressure on the Ulster Premier, Captain Terence O'Neill to do something about the general situation. After this apparent failure on the political front the committee did approach counsel for an opinion on the prospects of challenging the Dungannon Council on housing allocation, and received first a negative and then a guarded but reasonably favourable opinion, based on an assessment of the legal position by Harry Calvert of the Law Faculty of Queens University, Belfast. But when their application for legal aid to pursue the action was turned down by the Legal Aid Committee, and on appeal, the matter was not pursued. The Campaign for Social Justice clearly regarded this rebuff as further evidence of the essential bias in the system, and reverted to the view that, after six or seven years of effort with local lawyers, none of whom appeared to have any fire in their bellies, there was no future in legal redress.[3]

The simplest explanation for the persistence of this attitude was the feeling in Republican circles that the courts and the judiciary were part and parcel of the Unionist power structure and therefore unlikely to uphold any serious challenge to the regime. It is incontrovertible that the majority of judicial appointments in Northern Ireland have been made from the ranks of Unionism. Of twenty High Court judges appointed since the independent Northern Ireland courts were established, fifteen have been openly associated with the Unionist Party: of twenty-three County Court appointments, fourteen had been visibly connected with the Unionist administration. At the height of the civil rights campaign in the late 1960's two of the three judges in the Northern Ireland Court of Appeal were ex-Attorney-Generals in Unionist governments; one of the four High Court judges was likewise an ex-Attorney-General, and another the son of an Attorney-General; two of the five County Court judges were ex-Unionist M.P.s and another the son of a Unionist M.P.; and among the twelve Resident Magistrates there was an ex-Unionist M.P., an ex-Unionist Senator, a defeated Unionist candidate and a former legal adviser to the Ministry of Home Affairs.[4]

The significance of these political appointments can be overemphasised. There was an established tradition in all the jurisdictions of the British Isles, which has only recently been discarded, of raising ex-Attorney-Generals to the bench. Similar political affiliations of the kind alleged against Northern Ireland judges and magistrates could thus be raised against many judges in Britain and the Republic of Ireland.[5] But in Northern Ireland the permanent control of the Unionist Party at all levels of government lent a special force to complaints about political appointments. High Court appointments were the responsibility of the Westminster Government which clearly followed a policy of ensuring that at least one senior judicial appointment was held by a Roman Catholic. But this did not apply to county court or magistrates court appointments. Nor was there an opportunity for 'the other side' to restore the balance in its period of office as in other jurisdictions. Those members of the minority community who were appointed to judicial office were in any event regarded as 'Castle Catholics', more likely than not to support the government which had promoted them.

It does not follow from the preponderance of 'Unionists' on the bench in Northern Ireland that a challenge to the Unionist administration at central or local government level would necessarily fail. Adherence to the role of impartial judicial decision-making by 'political' appointees has sometimes led to remarkable changes in apparent political leanings.[6] There have been a number of cases in Northern Ireland in which ex-Unionist judges have taken a strong line against the executive (see pp. 30-35).

Nonetheless it can hardly be doubted that the composition of the judiciary did have an adverse effect on the confidence of the minority in the prospects of mounting a successful civil rights challenge in the courts. And when a case was finally raised on the banning of 'Republican Clubs' under the Special Powers Act, this assessment was apparently fully borne out. Whether this decision is to be attributed to political bias or to legal doctrine is a matter of debate. The performance of the Northern Ireland High Court judges in subsequent civil rights cases, in which challenges to the executive have regularly been upheld, would be sufficient to dispel a charge of any continuing political bias to any reasonably objective observer. But by then the spotlight of world attention had been focussed on Northern Ireland, the reality of complaints of gerrymandering and discrimination had been officially recognised and a programme of reforms initiated. The importance of the Republican Clubs affair as a test case on the practicability of pursuing the civil rights campaign through the courts cannot be overestimated.

**The Republican Clubs Case**

In March 1967, the Ministry of Home Affairs made a regulation under the Special Powers Act adding to the list of unlawful associations: "The organisations at the date of this regulation or at any time thereafter describing themselves as 'republican clubs' or any like organisation howsoever described". The addition appears to have been made in response to the growing civil rights agitation in traditionally Republican circles as an indication that the government would stand no nonsense from that quarter. But no serious attempt was made to enforce the regulation either on its introduction or subsequently.[7] The only case arising from the ban was in the nature of a test case against a Mr. McEldowney who was charged in March 1968 with being a member of the Slaughtneil Republican Club. It seems certain that the prosecution was initiated by the authorities in order to test the legality of the regulation. No similar action was taken against any other Republican Club and this case was taken to the House of Lords. The local magistrates dismissed the charge on the ground that the club in question could not be held to be unlawful as constituting a threat to peace and order in Northern Ireland within the terms of the regulation as they interpreted it. The Northern Ireland Court of Appeal reversed this decision on the ground that it was for the Minister of Home Affairs alone to decide whether a particular organisation should be deemed to be unlawful. But the Lord Chief Justice of Northern Ireland, Lord MacDermott, gave a strong dissenting judgement on the ground that the regulation as a whole was far too vague and wide to be capable of being related to the purpose prescribed in the Special Powers Act as being necessary for preserving peace and maintaining order in Northern Ireland. It is noteworthy that though one of the majority judges was a 'political' appointment in the sense of having been a Unionist Attorney General, the dissenting judge Lord MacDermott had been in exactly the same position.

The case came before the House of Lords in London in April 1969, and the appeal was dismissed by a majority of three law lords to two on 18th June. The majority held that in the absence of proof of bad faith, which was not alleged, it was for the Minister alone to decide on the subversive nature of any organisation, and that in the circumstances the words 'or any like organisation howsoever described' were not too wide to be supported. Lord Justice Diplock and Lord Justice Pearce dissented on similar grounds to those argued by Lord MacDermott, that since the magistrates had found as a fact that the Slaughtneil Republican Club had no seditious pursuits, a finding based on evidence given by the local police, it could not be argued that Republican Clubs as a class had unlawful objects; they further argued that the use of the words 'or any other like organisation howsoever described' rendered the regulation so vague as to fall outside the powers delegated to the Minister by the Act.[8]

The decision of the House of Lords in this case was in line with the prevailing British approach to constitutional law in refusing to challenge ministerial discretion in the absence of clear proof of bad faith. But in the context of Northern Ireland it was the final proof to the minority community that they could expect no aid from Britain in their struggle for what they regarded as their legitimate civil rights. Whether there was any element of political bias in the majority judgement either in the Northern Ireland Court of Appeal or even in the House of Lords must remain a matter of opinion. But there can be no doubt of its symbolic importance in showing the futility of pursuing the civil rights campaign through the courts. It is significant that the forces of law and order in Derry and Belfast broke down within weeks of the final rejection of the claim in the House of Lords.

**Subsequent civil rights legislation: the reform programme**

The violence of August 1969 and the arrival of British troops inevitably shifted the focus of attention away from internal civil rights litigation. Northern Ireland became a major political issue in the British Parliament and in the Republic of Ireland. The UK and Northern Ireland premiers met in London and issued a joint declaration confirming the constitutional position of Northern Ireland as part of the United Kingdom and thus the ultimate responsibility of the United Kingdom Government, and affirming the right of its citizens, irrespective of political views or religion, to the same equality of treatment and freedom from discrimination in all legislation and executive decisions of government as obtained in the rest of the United Kingdom.[9] Agreement was also reached on the broad outlines of a reform programme based on these principles.

The basis of this programme was not the creation of legally enforceable rights but the setting up of new or reformed institutions and agencies. The structure of the police force and the special constabulary was to be reviewed by leading British police chiefs; the reform of local government, incorporating universal adult franchise and an independent commission responsible for electoral boundaries, was to be pressed through; and equality of opportunity on public employment and fairness in the allocation of public housing was to be guaranteed by the appointment of parliamentary and local government ombudsmen. It was also agreed that it was vital that the momentum of these internal reforms be maintained.

It may be that these measures would have been sufficient to meet the legitimate complaints of the Roman Catholic community, though there were some important omissions, notably on discrimination in private employment. But the pace and manner of implementation was certainly not sufficient to gain their confidence or meet their expectations. As 1969 and 1970 dragged on with little outward sign of any improvement on any of the main civil rights issues protest marches and rioting continued on a sporadic basis. Confrontations with troops and police became more and more frequent in the Catholic enclaves of Belfast and Derry. There was a progressive escalation in the violence of the tactics employed by both sides. There was a corresponding shift in attention from social and economic issues to allegations of maltreatment by the security forces, culminating in the Lower Falls curfew of August 1970 and the internment and interrogation operation of August 1971. This was accompanied by the rebirth of militant Republicanism and organised guerrilla activity by persons whose main objective was not social and economic reform but the pursuit of Irish nationalism and the abolition of partition. This process and the response of the legal system to it is traced in the next chapter.

Continued support for the various protests and demonstrations from which these confrontations developed, and even sympathy for the guerrilla activists who eventually emerged, was nonetheless dependent on the persistent feeling among members of the minority community that their social and economic rights were being denied. It is important therefore to consider why the reform programme failed to win the confidence of those whom it was intended to benefit.

**The Failure of the Reform Programme to win the confidence of the minority**

The principal factor in this was perhaps the long delay in the implementation of the reform of local government. The fierce political battle between the two wings of the Unionist Party over this issue gave substance to the view that the Unionists would not willingly grant any reforms which would be any more than token gestures.

A number of leading Catholics, for instance, issued a statement in September 1971, following the internment operation, questioning whether any Unionist government could be entrusted with the introduction and implementation of a reform programme, and alleging that "the continued application of the Brookeborough formula of government by discrimination was maintaining intact the Unionist position of power."[10] It is easy to understand this feeling, given that the Unionist Party at that time were still in control of a number of local authority councils though their supporters were clearly a minority of the electorate, and that arrangements for a completely new and patently fair system would not be ready for implementation until 1973. The only action which had been taken in this field in the two years following on the violence of 1968 and 1969 was the replacement of the patently gerrymandered Londonderry Corporation by a non-elected Commission. Though the work of the Commission has been broadly praised, it remained a fact that control over local government was still denied to the elected representatives of the Roman Catholic community in areas where they were clearly in a majority.

A similar point may be made in relation to the reform of public housing. This had always been one of the most emotional issues in the civil rights campaign. Unionist councils, it was alleged, reserved the bulk of the better new houses for their own supporters. The validity of this claim has been contested on a statistical basis on the ground that overall the Catholic community did obtain a larger proportional share of public housing resources than the Protestant community, but more detailed analysis of the housing and census returns suggests that in Unionist controlled areas Protestants were given a disproportionate share of new houses.[11] The Cameron Commission concluded that there had been discrimination:

> We have no doubt . . . , in the light of the mass of evidence put before us, that in these Unionist-controlled areas it is fairly frequent for housing policy to be operated so that houses allocated to Catholics tended . . . to go to rehouse slum dwellers, whereas Protestant allocations tended to go more frequently to new families.[12]

Nor can it be doubted that some Unionist controlled local councils did make use of their control over housing to perpetuate their electoral advantage by allocating their own supporters in such a way as to maintain control over marginal wards, and ensuring that their more numerous opponents were safely gathered together in one or two predominantly Roman Catholic estates. The Cameron Commission concluded:

> Council housing policy has also been distorted for political ends in the Unionist controlled areas . . . In each, houses have been built and allocated in such a way that they will not disturb the political balance.[13]

The strategy for reform in housing was one of centralisation. In terms of administrative convenience and efficiency, and of staffing in an increasingly specialised profession, this policy can scarcely be contested. And although there was the expected delay in implementing the plan, so that the new central Housing Executive did not begin to take over the public housing functions of local councils until 1972, the proposed scheme was broadly welcomed in all quarters. In the meantime a fair points system was to be operated in all districts, though the spirit of the scheme was not always adhered to.[14] But once again the net effect of centralisation was to leave the balance of control over housing allocation in the hands of the representatives of the majority community who naturally outnumbered those of the minority on the new central authority. This is not to say that the new authority has been accused of improper practices or discriminatory allocation. But at the lower levels of administration many of the old familiar faces continue to confront those who apply for new or exchanged tenancies, and the local representatives of the Roman Catholic community were until May 1973 no more in control in Roman Catholic areas than ever they were.

**The Ombudsmen**

It is in this context of continuing control of local government in most areas by the established Unionist Councils that the performance of other less far-reaching elements in the reform programme should be judged. Ombudsmen with wide powers to scrutinise the decisions of both central and local government agencies had been promised in the initial reform packages of November 1968 and September 1969 respectively. The Northern Ireland Parliamentary Commissioner of Administration covering central government, and the Commissioner for Complaints, a similar office in respect of local government, were appointed without undue delay in July 1969 and December 1969 respectively and went to work immediately on a large number of outstanding complaints. Reports on their first completed investigations followed soon after. But in neither case did the new system make much impact, and there were no forthright revelations of the kinds of blatant discrimination which the Roman Catholic community had come to believe were widespread.

There are a number of factors which may help to explain this lack of impact. In the first place the actual extent of blatant discrimination had been somewhat exaggerated. Both the Parliamentary Commissioner and the Commissioner for Complaints reported favourably on the generally high standard of administration in central and local government. Furthermore many of the most publicised cases of imbalance between Unionist and non-Unionist representatives on public bodies and in senior civil service posts could be attributed to the disinclination of some Roman Catholics in earlier years to become involved in the institutions of a state to which they preferred not to give their recognition and support. In the second place, the Commissioners were barred by their terms of reference from doing anything about cases of discrimination which arose from decisions made prior to the establishment of their offices. Nor were they in a position to do anything about established patterns of discrimination, in particular in local government employment and housing. Their terms of reference were directed to the scrutiny of individual decisions rather than the overall percentages of employees or housing allocations among members of the two religious and political communities. Even in respect of current decisions it was, in any case, virtually impossible to establish conclusively that improper factors had been taken into account given the accepted tradition of tacit understanding in matters of this kind in Northern Ireland. The Commissioner for Complaints commented openly in his second report on the difficulty of obtaining information about the numbers of Protestants and Roman Catholics employed in the bodies with which he was concerned.[15]

In any event the Commissioners failed to reveal any noteworthy cases of discrimination in the early years of their work. And yet there were a number of highly publicised cases of just the kind of apparently blatant discrimination — notably over the non-appointment of a Mr. Doherty to a post with the Londonderry Commission on the direction of the Ministry of Development[16] — with which the new agencies were intended to deal.

Finally, and perhaps most important, the Commissioners were debarred from dealing with cases of discrimination at the most serious political level. For instance in the widely publicised case of a decision by a Protestant Rural District Council to refuse permission to the local Roman Catholic Gaelic League to make use of the Council's playing fields for their traditional Sunday matches, the Commissioner held that he could not in the absence of any procedural irregularities consider the merits of the decision itself. Similarly, the Commissioner felt himself debarred from interfering in cases where the allegation was of communal rather than individual discrimination. In one publicised case concerning the alleged failure of a local authority to provide health and welfare facilities in a predominantly Roman Catholic area, the Commissioner informed the complainant that "The Act under which he operated . . . was intended essentially to provide a means whereby the complaints of an individual citizen who felt he had been unfairly treated by a local or public authority could be investigated; it was not intended to deal with issues affecting equally the whole general public in a large area."[17] Yet it was precisely this kind of large scale discrimination which had been central to the allegations of the civil rights campaigners.

It is thus scarcely surprising that the activists in the minority community refused to believe that they could expect any real assistance from the new agencies. The Commissioners did have, and continue to have, some measure of success in dealing with minor cases of administrative tangles and insensitivity, in which their intervention is crucial to the working out of a satisfactory settlement. But their political impact has been minimal. Whether this was due to a lack of zeal in rooting out the real reasons underlying contested decisions and relentlessly pursuing any matters raised to the limit of their express powers, or to a defect in the formulation of the powers and duties of the new agencies, must remain a matter of opinion. But it would be difficult to argue convincingly that the new ombudsmen have done the job that they were ostensibly appointed to do.

**The Police**

A similar comment may be made in respect of the structural reform of the police. Following the recommendations of the Hunt Report in October 1968, the paramilitary B Specials were disbanded and replaced by the part-time Ulster Defence Regiment under British Army command. The Royal Ulster Constabulary was also to be reconstituted as a wholly civilian and non-armed force on the British model under the control of a widely representative Police Authority. The continuing violence and the growth of guerrilla activity effectively thwarted the achievement of the first objective. And the new Police Authority failed to assert itself in such a way as to alter the public conception of the police force as an agent of the Unionist Government. For example, in one of its early decisions on the highly emotive question of marching, the Authority was equally divided on a decision to ban a particular march. The Chairman who had the casting vote suggested that instead of using it the decision should be referred back to the Minister of Home Affairs. This was accepted. Here again the reform programme, whatever its intentions, clearly failed to achieve any change in public attitudes to established institutions.

**Subsequent civil rights cases**

Two further cases of a civil rights character which were finally pursued in the courts should also be mentioned. Both originated in Dungannon under the general auspices of the Campaign for Social Justice. The first was brought against the Dungannon RDC in respect of alleged discrimination in the allocation of houses in a new council estate. The case came before Mr. Justice Gibson early in 1971. On any objective assessment his judgement on the case could only be taken as a qualified victory for the complainants: "The failure of the defendants to allot a proportion only of the houses to incoming workers, the enlargement of that class beyond its legitimate bounds and the priority of allocation given to them would operate to reduce the number of houses available to other applicants to a degree which could cause considerable hardship in some cases and constitutes an illegitimate operation of the [points] scheme". And he gave an informal direction to the Council to consider the allocation of the disputed houses "in accordance with the principles which he had stated rather than in the manner in which they had hitherto acted."[18] Nonetheless, the introduction to the judge's reasoned judgement was one-sided:

> Before becoming involved in the details of the case, I think I should state at the outset my clear conclusion that the evidence of such lettings as were considered did not at all indicate that the Defendants selected tenants for houses in a capricious way or from motives of discrimination, or that the applications of persons who were not supporters of the Unionist Majority in the Council suffered by having their claims deliberately deferred or overlooked.

This states only part of the final conclusion to the case. The evidence did not establish impropriety; nor did it establish that there was no impropriety. It was this introduction which caused the local press to report that the judge had cleared the Council of any impropriety. This may have been influential in the decision not to take the case further.

The second case was brought against the Dungannon Urban District Council over the failure to pursue a redevelopment scheme in the way suggested by a Ministry inspector allegedly with the object of injuring local Roman Catholic business opportunities. Here too the case came before Mr. Justice Gibson in April 1971, and was rejected on the ground that the issue could not be decided on affidavit evidence alone, prior to the trial of the case on the evidence of relevant witnesses. Whether the evidence of witnesses would have been sufficient was never tested, since the case was not pursued further.

**Conclusion**

A number of comments may be made on these cases in particular, and on the legal response to the civil rights campaign in general. First, it is doubtful whether the prevalent style of legal decision making, in which cases are dealt with on the basis of very precise and often highly technical issues rather than the broad issues underlying the dispute, is appropriate in civil rights litigation. This approach is perhaps more attractive to the judges, in that it enables them to side-step the main issues. But all too often it has meant that the courts have not fulfilled their main function which is precisely to deal with these main issues insofar as they are subject to legal adjudication. When the guarantors of civil rights take refuge in technicalities, aggrieved complainants are more likely to take to the streets.

The second point is closely related, and concerns the unwillingness of some judges to make the kind of condemnation of unlawful or improper practices which in simple terms will hit the headlines. Even in cases which have effectively been won, as in the first Dungannon case, the careful language of the judgement permitted the decision to be portrayed as a vindication of the errant defendant. Public confidence in the courts as the ultimate and impartial guarantors of freedom and justice within the law requires a much more open approach to speech writing than has been traditional in British legal circles. It is notable that since the introduction of internment, the judiciary has in fact adopted a much more forceful stance on civil liberties, and public confidence has increased accordingly. But any beneficial effect has been lost by the superimposition of extra-legal powers, which is discussed in detail in the next chapter.

A similar comment may be made about the work of the new anti-discrimination agencies. Neither the Parliamentary Commissioner nor the Commissioner for Complaints has been prepared to make the kind of forthright condemnation of Unionist power structures which the minority wanted. Some of the factors which lay behind this failure have already been discussed. But the low-key style in which the Commissioners approached their work was perhaps as important as any of the more formal restraints imposed on them by their terms of reference. The obligation imposed on the Commissioners to preserve complete confidentiality in their investigations and reports was clearly a crucial factor in this context. But there is no indication that this was an unwelcome restriction in the eyes of those concerned. The pace and language of the British civil service tradition which has been consistently followed by the Commissioners was as inappropriate as the technicality of the British legal system as a means of building up confidence in the organs of government in a divided community.

These criticisms of the courts and the new ombudsmen, however, must be set in the broader context of the situation in Northern Ireland. Discrimination was and remains a structural problem created over a period of many years of decision-making affecting both individual job appointments and the allocation of public resources. The imbalance in the proportion of Roman Catholics and Protestants in senior civil service and local government posts could not have been corrected overnight by any form of judicial or quasi-judicial supervision or control. Nor could major decisions taken in the past, such as the siting of the New University in Coleraine rather than Londonderry, allegedly for political rather than academic reasons, or the concentration of economic development in the predominantly Protestant area east of the River Bann (though here there were probably more apparently valid though politically shortsighted reasons for the decision), be corrected by judicial review alone even if they had been open to independent scrutiny. No amount of civil rights litigation or review could of itself have solved the problems created by political bias. Nonetheless the courts and later the ombudsmen failed to bring these issues into the open in such a way as to assist in the political reform process.

## References


1. *Disturbances in Northern Ireland,* Cmd 532, Belfast 1969, para. 229.
2. *Constitutional Law in Northern Ireland* by Harry Calvert, Stevens 1968, pp. 334-335.
3. For a further description of the attempts to seek redress in the courts by the Campaign for Social Justice, see 'The Search for Justice in Northern Ireland' by W. Don Carroll, *New York University Journal of International Law and Politics*, Vol. 6, Spring 1973.
4. These figures are taken from the researches of Kevin Boyle of Queen's University, Belfast. See *Fortnight*, 3rd June 1971.
5. See for example, *In Search of Justice,* by Brian Abel Smith and Robert Stevens, Allen Lane 1968, Chapter 6.
6. For example, there have been surprising changes in judicial attitudes on the part of judges appointed to the United States Supreme Court.
7. The ban was lifted in March 1973.
8. *McEldowney v Forde* [1969] 3 W.L.R. 179.
9. *Northern Ireland: Text of a Communique and Declaration issued after a meeting held at 10 Downing Street on August 19th, 1969,* Cmnd. 4154.
10. *Commentary upon the White Paper (Command Paper 558) entitled 'A Record of Constructive Change'*, Belfast 1971.
11. See *Governing Without Consensus* by Richard Rose, Faber 1971, and the criticisms of it in *Housing in Northern Ireland* by W.D. Birrell et. al., Centre for Environmental Studies, University Working Paper 12, 1971, p. 149.
12. Cmd. 532, para 140.
13. Cmd. 532, para 139.
14. In his annual report for 1972 the Commissioner for Complaints referred to three cases of maladministration of housing allocation by a local authority in which "the members, on the last occasion on which they were in a position to exercise powers of allocation under the Housing Acts, appeared to have decided to have a 'last fling'." H.C. 158, Belfast 1973, para. 31.
15. *Second Report of the Northern Ireland Commissioner for Complaints,* H.C. 2048. Belfast 1970, para 53.
16. *Fortnight* No. 9, 22 January 1971.
17. *Fortnight* No. 10, 5 February 1971.
18. *Fortnight* No. 14, 2 April 1971, *Campbell & Casey v Dungannon RDC,* 19 March 1971.

CHAPTER III

# From Civil Rights to Guerrilla Warfare

The slide from peaceful protest into guerrilla warfare in Northern Ireland was a gradual process which stretched from the summer of 1968 up to the introduction of internment in August 1971. As the process continued there was a corresponding change in the primary focus of attention from civil rights to law and order, from protection from discrimination to protection from physical violence by terrorists or security forces. The legal response to these new problems, however, was no more successful than to those of discrimination. The rest of this study is an attempt to explain this failure of law and lawyers to stem the descent into communal and military conflict. Before dealing with the specifically legal issues which have arisen in this phase of the Northern Ireland crisis a brief general account will be given of the background to the slide into violence and terrorism. Three major factors can perhaps be isolated by way of explanation.

The first was the build up of a sense of frustration in the Roman Catholic community at the failure of their attempts to achieve any real progress by political agitation alone. Significantly this feeling of frustration was particularly strong in Londonderry, where serious violence first broke out. Following the recession of 1965 a newly founded and government assisted factory closed down, throwing some 2,000 men out of work. With the continuing decline in the traditional textile and shirt-making industry this raised the unemployment rate in the city to more than 10%. About the same time the final decisions were made to move the county administrative offices from Londonderry, the natural capital, to the predominantly Protestant centre of Coleraine in the east of the county, and to establish the proposed New University of Ulster there. These three decisions were seen as final proof that the Unionist Government were prepared to jettison Londonderry, which despite its significance in Orange history could not be 'held' indefinitely given the two to one majority of Roman Catholics in the population. All this occurred in a period when for the first time the Nationalist Party had decided to take an active part in local government. Similar feelings in other centres, like Dungannon and Newry and West Belfast, where active political representation by a new generation of capable non-Unionist M.P.s had likewise failed to produce any substantial results, set the scene for the mass support for the initial peaceful marches and demonstrations and later for more militant action and rioting. As none of the allegedly discriminatory decisions which were contested during this period were later altered, this feeling of frustration continued throughout the period of emergency.

The second factor was the increasingly violent reaction in the Protestant community to the civil rights campaign. For a long period this was centred on the colourful but supposedly irrelevant antics of Ian Paisley and his band of religious and political supporters, though there had been flare-ups of more serious sectarian violence, notably in the Malvern Street murder affair of 1966 and the Cromac Square and Divis Street disturbances in Belfast. But as the civil rights campaign moved into the phase of public demonstrations and protests the determination of the Protestant militants to interfere with civil rights marches and meetings, and where possible to prevent their occurrence, became more and more apparent. Attacks by Protestant extremists on civil rights supporters in Dungannon in August, November and December 1968, in Armagh in November 1970 and in Londonderry in January 1969 are fully documented in the report of the Cameron Commission.

The official response of the Unionist Government, under the direction of the Minister of Home Affairs, William Craig, to the civil rights campaign was likewise openly repressive. A blanket ban on 'Republican Clubs' in any form had been introduced under the Special Powers Act at the very beginning of the active phase of the civil rights campaign, though this was as much a symbolic as a real measure of oppression. More practically, the government adopted an increasingly restrictive attitude to civil rights demonstrations and marches. Marches and counter marches have always been a problem in Northern Ireland, and the authorities have wide powers both under the Public Order Acts and the Special Powers Act to control the route of proposed marches or to ban them altogether. The necessity for some power to control demonstrations can scarcely be contested given the practice among opponents of any particular faction of organising or threatening an opposing march or demonstration on the same route. But equally, it can hardly be doubted that in the early phases of the civil rights campaign the powers were used in a partisan fashion.

The most notorious example of this was the banning of the civil rights march proposed for October 1968 in Londonderry because an allegedly traditional Apprentice Boys parade was threatened. The Cameron Commission found this to have been devised specially for the occasion.[1] The net effect in the opinion of the Cameron Commission was an increase in support for the march and in the militancy of many of the marchers. But it was undoubtedly the violent attack by the police on the marchers, widely recorded on television and by the press, which more than any other event convinced the people of Derry that the government was committed to a policy of repression rather than reform.

From then on it became increasingly difficult to distinguish between official and unofficial reactionary violence, at least for the Roman Catholic community. Large numbers of the 'B Special' constabulary were undoubtedly involved, though in a private capacity, in the organised ambush on the People's Democracy march from Belfast to Londonderry at Burntollet in January 1969. The ensuing riotous confrontations in Londonderry in January and April were followed by two night-time 'invasions' of the Roman Catholic Bogside area by large numbers of uniformed RUC officers in the course of which substantial damage and injury to residents and property was inflicted. Final confirmation for the minority community of the unity of purpose between the RUC, the B Specials and the

Protestant militants was given by the events of August 1969 in Londonderry, Armagh, Coalisland, Dungannon, Dungiven and Belfast, which finally led to the deployment of British forces. Detailed analysis of these events is beyond the scope of this study. The report of the Scarman Tribunal concluded that the RUC was in the main a non-partisan force caught between two sets of militants bent on violent confrontation, a victim of circumstances and its own faulty intelligence, rather than a willing participant in the violence.[2] But it is a fact that the RUC failed to prevent large numbers of houses on the fringes of Roman Catholic areas in Belfast from being burnt out. And the action of the few 'Black Sheep' in the force and the failure of their superior officers either to control them in advance or discipline them after the event reduced still further the confidence of the minority in the impartiality of the RUC.

The third factor was the growing conflict between British troops and the Provisional IRA. This was a seemingly inexorable and self-perpetuating process. British troops were brought in to act as peace-keepers between the two communities in August 1969, when the local police and the B Specials could no longer contain the situation. The arrival of the soldiers was widely welcomed by the Roman Catholic community as a guarantee against further Protestant attacks. But Army commanders were aware that their men were not trained for or suited to a long term peace-keeping role, and issued frequent statements on the need for a political solution. These fears proved amply justified. It is now widely accepted that in the summer of 1969 the IRA existed as a serious military force only in the files of the RUC special branch, and in the imagination of leading Unionist politicians.[3] The development of genuine guerrilla potential and of the will to take on the British Army was the result of a series of political and military blunders by the British, and from support and encouragement of traditional Republican activists from the South.

The first moves to rebuild the IRA were almost wholly defensive.[4] Emissaries were sent to Dublin in the late summer of 1969 to seek assistance for the protection of the Roman Catholic enclaves in Belfast. They were given both arms and money, some of it diverted under highly disputed circumstances from the official government funds voted by the Dail for the relief of those who had suffered in the North.[5] Local defence groups and vigilante forces were set up to man the barricades, and prepare for any new onslaughts. Senior Army officers were careful to keep up a direct line of communication with these groups in the months that followed the British intervention. But as the exasperation of the ordinary soldiers increased at the endless confrontations and riots, whose underlying causes they could not understand, and the pressures from Unionist politicians for a tougher Army line with rioters grew, so the downward spiral of antagonism between soldiers and the Roman Catholic communities in Londonderry and Belfast gathered pace.

At the start there were minor incidents of verbal abuse and harassment, especially in the case of those Scottish regiments which were regarded as particularly partial to the Protestant cause. Increasingly the stones and bottles of the rioters were replaced by petrol bombs and grenades, and the batons and barbed wire of the soldiers by CS gas and rubber bullets. The confrontation reached disastrous proportions in the Lower Falls curfew of July 1970, which followed almost accidentally from a routine arms search. Then there were the first fatal shooting of a rioter, the killing of Daniel O'Hagan in the New Lodge Road area of Belfast in 1970, and the first Army fatality at the hands of the IRA in February 1971. During the spring and summer of 1971 the IRA Provisional activists encouraged and organised young rioteers in Ballymurphy and the Bogside and then moved in with weapons and explosives themselves, in the hope of provoking the soldiers into unjustifiable action, which could then be used as justification for further confrontations. This policy was extremely successful. The fatal shootings of Beattie and Cusack in Londonderry in July 1971 in circumstances which gave some justification to the Army, but not enough to silence the demands for an inquiry, led to the withdrawal of the opposition party from the Stormont Parliament and thus to the failure of the policy of pressing for a political settlement by gradual means.

By this time the Provisional IRA had clearly built itself into a strong and well organised military force with a fair measure of tacit support in the main Roman Catholic enclaves. The introduction of internment in August 1971 completed the process. The list of those arrested and detained was so out of date and haphazard, and the treatment meted out in the detention and interrogation centres, as reported by the Compton Tribunal[6] and in subsequent legal proceedings, so harsh as to unite the Roman Catholic community in Northern Ireland behind the Provisionals as never before. Recruitment and financial support are reported to have risen dramatically on both sides of the border, and the phase of all-out guerrilla warfare began in earnest. In the seven months prior to the introduction of internment in August 1971 12 soldiers were killed; from September to December in that year 40 members of the security forces were killed. The initial reaction to internment was then maintained by the continuing harassment and arrests in the Roman Catholic areas and by a series of disputed incidents in which allegedly innocent civilians were shot by Army patrols. There have been ups and downs in the intensity of the IRA campaign, and in the degree of support or opposition from Roman Catholics following the various political and military incidents: Bloody Sunday in January 1972, Direct Rule in March 1972, Bloody Friday in July 1972, the period of sectarian assassinations in summer 1972, the White Paper in March 1973. The number of persons interned has fluctuated accordingly from a maximum of 900 to a minimum of 200 and back up to 400. There have also been periods in which the main focus has been on Protestant militancy in response to political moves or military incidents in Protestant areas. But the Provisional IRA and the British Army are still pursuing their war with determination and zeal.

Various explanations may be offered for the progression of events. There was the failure of the social and economic reform programme to bring about any observable change in conditions in the Roman Catholic enclaves in which the Provisional IRA is based. There was the failure of the various political initiatives to produce a broadly acceptable settlement under which ordinary political activity could resume. But the single most important factor was perhaps the behaviour of the British Army. There was always a danger that the close proximity of the troops and civilians in the rougher areas of Belfast and Derry would lead to trouble. In the Ballymurphy area of Belfast, for example, where most of the initial confrontations took place in the early months of 1970, it was not long before the friendly tea-sipping days of the initial reception gave way to accusations of unnecessary force by soldiers in dealing with riotous youngsters. The army in turn began to lose patience at the numerous conflicting roles which they were called on to perform. The risk that the minor confrontations which naturally developed would escalate into a more serious conflict was obvious. But there were a number of specific factors which help to explain the process.

First, senior Army officers and politicians failed to appreciate the frustrations and fears of the Roman Catholic community. They failed also to realise the extent of the antagonism which was developing between the ordinary soldiers and the Roman Catholic population. As a result no adequate measures were taken to prevent or minimise the conflict which developed.

Second, the Army was untrained in peace-keeping. Its experience was principally in the techniques of conventional warfare. This gave rise to a number of problems when it came to Northern Ireland. To begin with the standard weapons and procedures of military action were inappropriate for the tasks of crowd and riot control. The situation was particularly confusing for the soldier on the ground because he did not have an identifiable enemy and was confronted daily by people of the same class as himself, who spoke the same language. Soldiers were further confused by the fact that the same individuals who were friendly to them at one part of the day would throw bottles and stones at them at another.

Third, the nature of the Army as a closed institution increased the likelihood that individual soldiers would not keep strictly to the rule of law. They knew that there was a major propaganda effort to show how effectively the security forces were dealing with the disorders. And they realised that any breaches in discipline would be effectively concealed either by their own colleagues or by the bureaucratic nature of the Army command.[7]

Finally, whether on their own initiative, or more probably as a result of political pressure from the Unionist Government, the Army began to adopt a tougher attitude towards rioting from about February 1970. They also intensified their searches for arms in the Roman Catholic community, without undertaking similar operations in Protestant areas. This inevitably led to greater antagonism between individual units and the large numbers of innocent people whose houses were 'ransacked' or who were subjected to inconvenience and harassment.

The contribution of all these factors and of other related elements in the situation to the downward spiral of confrontation and conflict could be plotted in detail. The primary concern in this study is the more limited one of explaining the failure of the legal system to operate as a brake on the process of escalation by substituting an acceptable means of settling both major and minor conflicts by non-violent means. For ease in analysis this will be dealt with at two levels: first in respect of what may be termed the pre-judicial operations of dealing with public disorder and terrorism, notably the powers of arrest, detention and questioning, and the problem of 'accidental' incidents in which allegedly innocent civilians have been shot; and secondly the operation of the formal judicial system itself in the course of the emergency. But it should be remembered that in terms of public confidence the legal system is perceived as a single whole.

**References**


1. Cmd. 532, para. 160.
2. *Violence and Civil Disturbances in Northern Ireland in 1969,* Cmd. 556, Belfast 1972, Chapter 3.
3. Cmd. 566, Chapter 3.8.
4. For a full account of the rebirth of the IRA, see *Ulster* by The Sunday Times Insight Team, Penguin 1972.
5. See the report of the Public Accounts Committee set up by the Parliament of the Republic of Ireland, P.R.L. 2574, Dublin 1972.
6. *Report of the enquiry into allegations against the security forces of physical brutality in Northern Ireland arising out of events on the 9th August, 1971,* Cmd. 4823, 1971.
7. This point is taken from an unpublished submission by Gill Boehringer to the Parker Committee on methods of interrogation.

## CHAPTER IV

# Civil Rights in an Emergency: Pre-Judicial Powers

The main legal issues which have arisen in respect of police and Army operations in Northern Ireland have not been the extent of the emergency powers but their abuse in individual incidents. From the time of the RUC assault on the Londonderry marchers in October 1968 and the subsequent police incursions into the Bogside to the present, attention has been focussed on allegations of misconduct and unlawful physical violence by the security forces. It would be tedious to attempt to list all of these incidents and difficult to deal with any of them conclusively, given the inevitable conflict of evidence and the lack of reliable first-hand accounts. The emphasis here will be on the general issue of how the undoubtedly widespread allegations of misconduct and unlawful violence have been dealt with by the authorities, and the effect on public confidence of the methods used.

### The Special Powers Act

The basis of police and Army powers in dealing with public disorder and terrorism since 1969 has been the Civil Authority (Special Powers) Act (Northern Ireland) 1922, commonly known as the Special Powers Act, and the numerous regulations made under it. This statute was originally introduced as a temporary measure to replace the Preservation of Order (Ireland) Act of 1918, but was continued on an annual basis until 1933 when it was rendered permanent. It confers wide powers of arrest, questioning, detention and internment on the security forces as agents of the civil authorities, and an almost completely unrestricted power to make regulations with the force of law, for instance to prescribe organisations, and to regulate the conduct of parades and funerals. Since Direct Rule the procedure for hearing appeals against internment has been altered by the Detention of Terrorists Order 1972, and the Special Powers Act itself has now been replaced by the Northern Ireland (Emergency Provisions) Act 1973. But the basic legal position has not been substantially altered.

The Special Powers Act was initially intended for use exclusively against Republican activists, and until the imposition of direct rule was so used with a few minor exceptions.[1] Its existence and the way in which it has been used have always been high on the list of grievances among the Roman Catholic community in Northern Ireland. But it has always been regarded as more or less unchallengeable in the courts. In an early case arising out of the arrest and detention of a prosperous hotel owner in Portadown in 1922, on the ground of his involvement in a conspiracy against the security of the newly created state of Northern Ireland, a charge which was virogously denied on behalf of the accused, the Northern Ireland High Court rejected an application for *habeas corpus* on the ground that it was within the power of the Minister of Home Affairs to make such detention and internment orders under the Act and that it was not for the court to express an opinion on the facts of the case.[2] This decision was regarded as incorrect by some leading authorities, notably by the editor of the second edition of Halsbury's Statutes[3] on the ground that an objective assessment of the facts was required under the terms of the Act and could be inquired into by the courts. But the futility of any legal challenge to individual decisions made under it was effectively confirmed by the decision of the House of Lords in the Republican Clubs case (see page 12) and by the action of the British Parliament in response to the decision in the Hume case. (See below page 31)

The Special Powers Act in fact constitutes a complete and effective abrogation of the rule of law. Under it the security authorities have always had the power to arrest and detain anyone they please without giving any reason and without fear of being called to account in respect of any decisions later shown to have been unjustified, as for instance in the case of many of those arrested and detained in the internment operation of August 1971 against whom, in the judgment of the Diplock Commission, 'suspicion was founded on inadequate and inaccurate information'.[4] In this sense Northern Ireland has always been and remains a permanent potential police state.

It should also be noted that where action under the Special Powers Act was legally doubtful or politically unattractive the security forces could always fall back on the common law. The curfew which was imposed in the Lower Falls area in August 1970 was later justified by a Belfast Magistrate in a test case brought against an individual for ignoring the restrictions on movement, on the ground that the Army commander was entitled in a situation of emergency to make what orders were necessary for the preservation of the peace.[5] Similarly in the case of the shooting of suspected terrorists, the rules laid down for individual soldiers in the 'Yellow Card' are no more than a reasonably accurate summary of the common law rules on the use of lethal force to protect oneself or others from armed attack or explosives, or to arrest persons reasonably suspected of being currently involved in offensive action. The lack of clarity on the extent of the common law in such cases has made the actions of the security forces even more difficult to assess or challenge effectively.

**The failure of inquiries**

At first the natural reaction to allegations of misconduct by the security forces was the call for, and occasionally the appointment of official judicial inquiries. Since 1969 there have been four major tribunals of inquiry into events in Northern Ireland: the Cameron Commission on Disturbances in Northern Ireland between October 1968 and March 1969[6]; the Scarman Tribunal on Violence and Civil Disturbances in Northern Ireland in 1969[7]; the Compton Inquiry into allegations against the security forces of physical brutality in Northern Ireland arising out of events on August 9th 1971[8]; and the Widgery Tribunal on events on

Sunday 30th January 1972 in Londonderry.[9] To these might be added the reports of the Parker Committee on Methods of Interrogation[10], the Diplock Committee on Legal Procedures to deal with Terrorist Activities[11], and the Scotland Yard investigation into the death of Samuel Devenny following the RUC incursions into the Bogside in April 1969.

Though there have been complaints from committed factions on the thoroughness of the investigation conducted in some of these cases, it can hardly be doubted that those concerned did a reasonably good job, at least in eliciting the basic facts of what happened in the incidents which they were inquiring into. But equally it can hardly be doubted that the various inquiries failed completely in what was presumably their prime function of restoring public confidence in the conduct of the security forces; alternatively, if their intended purpose was merely to deflect public concern in the hope that the inevitable delay of the inquiry process would reduce the impact of the allegations of misconduct, they certainly did not succeed in that either. Three broad reasons may be given for this failure.

In the first place the conclusions which the various reports drew from their findings, with the possible exception of Cameron and Scarman, were not always in accord with what might have been expected from an objective assessment of those findings. Compton based his assessment on the allegations of brutality on a thoroughly unconvincing distinction between brutality and ill-treatment. And Lord Widgery made a generally favourable assessment of the conduct of the Paratroops in Londonderry which it is difficult to justify in terms of the specific findings he made over the various individual incidents with which he was concerned, notably the 'reckless' shooting in the Glenfada Flats area. It was these overall assessments rather than the detailed findings which attracted the widespread reaction that the reports were merely 'whitewashing' the actions of the security forces. Assessments of this kind must remain a matter of opinion, but the Compton and Widgery reports certainly failed to persuade either the Roman Catholic community or uncommitted observers[12] that their assessments had struck the right balance.

Second, there was the question of delay. This applies primarily to the Scarman Tribunal which stretched over two whole years and finally reported nearly three years after the events into which it was inquiring. It is hardly surprising that after such a long delay the impact of the report in terms of restoring confidence in the impartiality of the RUC, insofar as that was a valid finding, was virtually nil. By that time an entirely new set of disputed incidents and allegations had taken over from those of 1969.

Finally, and perhaps most important, was the fact that no action was taken to deal with those cases in which the various reports found the security forces or individual soldiers or policemen to have been seriously at fault. The most notorious instances in this respect were the findings of ill-treatment/brutality against those involved in the arrest, detention and interrogation of some of the persons arrested in August 1971, and the finding over the Glenfada Flats incidents in which four civilians were shot dead, that on the balance of probability "when these four men were shot the group of civilians was not acting aggressively and that the shots were fired without justification".[13] It is widely agreed that in these cases the actions by the security forces constituted the criminal offences of assault or manslaughter, if not murder. Yet no proceedings were authorised by the Attorney General, despite a good deal of political pressure for such action to be taken. A similar comment may be made in respect of the equally serious findings by Cameron and Scarman in respect of RUC and 'B Special' conduct in the earlier period, notably in respect of the shooting of John Gallagher in Armagh in August 1969, and the assaults on Samuel Devenny in Londonderry in April 1969. Yet neither of these cases, which have always received particular attention in allegations against the security forces, nor the many more less serious cases of proven misconduct, have resulted in any public disciplinary action or sanctions against those responsible. Even when a full scale and independent police investigation was instituted, as in the Devenny case, the sole result was a report that a conspiracy of silence within the RUC was preventing those responsible from being identified. Moreover, the appointment of judges to chair what have turned out to be essential political inquiries, has blurred the distinction between executive and judicial functions, and has had an adverse effect on public confidence in the impartial role of the latter. The cumulative effect has undoubtedly been to destroy any feeling that may have existed that the appointment of an official inquiry would lead to justice being done.

**Defensive legal action**

The second phase in the response to alleged unlawful conduct by the security forces was the resort to legal action on behalf of those who claimed to have suffered injury or injustice. The initial impetus for this was undoubtedly provided by the internment and interrogation operations of August and September 1971, which had the effect of uniting the Roman Catholic community in opposition to current security policies. This brought general support from Roman Catholic lawyers to the idea of challenging the security forces in the courts. But much of the legal activity which has ensued may be traced to the operation of the Association for Legal Justice, a group of lawyers based in Belfast who have set out to encourage the use of legal processes to deal with allegations against the security forces and thus to help lessen the risk of direct retaliatory action against them. Two broad forms of action have been taken: first the use of procedural and technical defences based on misconduct by the security forces in cases where criminal charges have been brought against suspected terrorists; and secondly, the institution of direct civil and criminal proceedings against individual members of the security forces in respect of assaults, contested shooting incidents and other cases of unlawful activities by soldiers or the police. The record of the Northern Ireland judiciary in dealing with these cases has been such as to dispel any reasonable suspicion of bias in favour of the security forces. But in almost every case, as will be seen, the response of the executive authorities by way of 'remedial' action has been such that any possible beneficial effect in terms of public confidence in the courts has been wholly or largely destroyed.

The first actions taken were a direct challenge to the legality of the whole internment operation. *Habeas corpus* proceedings were instituted in London in August 1971 in respect of two of those who had been arrested in the internment swoop of August 1971 and who were detained at that time in the prison ship Maidstone in Belfast Lough. The main ground of complaint was that it was beyond the power of the civil authorities in Northern Ireland to authorise the British Army to make arrests by regulations issued under the Special Powers Act. These test cases first came before Ackner J. who accepted jurisdiction but refused the applications on the merits, on the ground that Regulation 11, permitting members of Her Majesty's forces to make arrests without warrant, could not be said to constitute an infringement of the ban imposed by the Government of Ireland Act 1920 on legislation by the Northern Ireland Parliament in respect of the armed forces.[14] This decision was effectively upheld on appeal, though on the different ground that the British courts had had no jurisdiction to hear *habeas corpus* applications from Ireland since 1782 or 1783.[15]

When these writs of *habeas corpus* were further pursued in the High Court in Northern Ireland, as suggested by the British Court of Appeal, reliance was placed on the alternative ground that the men had not been properly informed of the grounds for their arrest. (see page 32) But the challenge to the validity of regulations under the Special Powers Act conferring powers on the armed forces of the Crown was pursued in a later case, carefully selected for the purpose. The case arose out of the arrest of two Northern Ireland M.P.s for refusing to obey the order of an Army officer, purporting to act under a power to disperse any public assembly conferred on him by Regulation 38 of the Special Powers Act. The defendants, who had been engaged in a sit-down demonstration against the behaviour of British troops in Derry, were convicted by the local magistrate, but won their appeal in the Northern Ireland High Court which held that in purporting to confer powers on the British Army the regulation sought to achieve a lawful object by unlawful means.[16] This decision clearly raised substantial doubts as to the legality of many other actions by the British Army taken under the Special Powers Act. But the basis of the decision was immediately removed by the Westminster Parliament by the enactment within a matter of hours of the Northern Ireland Act 1972. This specifically authorised the Northern Ireland Parliament to legislate in respect of the armed forces of the Crown insofar as that was necesssary to the maintenance of peace and order in Northern Ireland, and conferred retrospective validity on any actions taken before the passing of the act which would otherwise have been invalid. But the general opinion that the Special Powers Act could not be effectively challenged had been upheld once again, despite the tactical victory won on the interpretation of the regulation in question. In addition the hope that some assistance in the campaign against the wide terms of the Special Powers Act could be expected from the British Parliament had been finally disappointed.

The unchallengeable character of the Special Powers Act, however, did not prevent a number of other tactical victories based on ordinary common law rights being won on behalf of persons arrested and detained, or charged with criminal offences. The application for *habeas corpus* which had been originated in London was eventually granted in the Northern Ireland High Court on the ground that the applicant had not on his arrest been properly informed of the legal basis for that arrest as is required at common law: simply to inform him that he was being arrested under the Special Powers Act was not sufficient since his rights, if any, and his opportunity, if any, to meet and challenge the right of arrest exercised against him, differed in accordance with which Regulation he was arrested under.[17] Since the identical form of words had been used by the Army in the case of all those arrested and detained during August and September, this decision clearly meant that all the arrests were similarly unlawful.

The practical effect of the decision in McElduff's case, however, was less far-reaching than might appear. There was nothing to prevent the authorities from remedying the technical defect by formally arresting all those concerned. Mr. McElduff himself was formally released by order of the court, but was rearrested and detained on leaving Belfast Prison. The net result in most cases was thus merely to open the way for a civil action against the authorities for unlawful imprisonment for the period of the unlawful detention. In one test case involving the unlawful detention of a young unmarried student for just over a month it was held that a sum of £400 would be adequate compensation.[18] In another bizarre case involving a criminal charge of escaping from prison it was held that the invalidity of the accused person's arrest necessarily destroyed the basis of the charge, since to escape from unlawful custody was not an offence.[19] But the more immediate and emotive issue of the continued detention of those concerned was not affected.

The positive effect of a number of other tactical legal victories in the period following the internment and interrogation operations may similarly be questioned. The judges of the High Court have not hesitated to apply the common law as to the admissibility of confessions to exclude any statements obtained by improper pressures on those accused. In one case the authorities admitted that the defendant had been kept in a tiny cubicle with room only for a wooden chair and questioned at intervals throughout the day and night for a period of twenty four hours. The judge rejected any allegations of physical-ill-treatment but held that: "the circumstances in which this accused was detained and which preceded the making of this statement were such as to sap that free will which must exist before a confession is voluntary", and refused to admit the statement.[20] In another case in which the facts are not reported the Lord Chief Justice refused to admit confessions on the ground that "the interrogation set-up was officially organised and operated in order to obtain information from persons who would otherwise have been less willing to give it."[21]

Procedural decisions of this kind have frequently resulted in directed acquittals or the withdrawal of formal charges against accused persons. The Attorney-Gen-General stated in Parliament in April 1973 that "there have been 55 abandoned cases, *nolle prosequis,* in Belfast since the beginning of 1972 mainly because of the inadmissibility of confession statements"; he also referred to 39 cases in which charges of possession of arms or explosives were withdrawn or the defendants discharged because of the technical rule that where premises are shared by several persons the prosecution must prove conclusively which of those persons was responsible for, or at least knew of, the presence of the arms or explosives.[22]

These defence victories, however, have not always led to the release of the defendant. There have been numerous cases in which the power to arrest and detain under the Special Powers Act has been used to 'correct' what may be viewed by the authorities as merely technical defeats. The most striking of these have been those in which persons who have been acquitted or discharged on all charges against them have been rearrested at the doors of the court. (See further below p. 55) This was also done in February 1972 to a man who had won an appeal against his original conviction on the ground of a misdirection to the jury. Court decisions on bail have also been set at nought by the authorities. In one well publicised case a Resident Magistrate decided that there was no case to answer on six of the seven charges brought against a Mr. Close in respect of a shooting incident some weeks prior to his arrest in August 1971, and ordered his release on bail; yet Mr. Close was immediately taken back into custody under the existing (and technically invalid) detention order against him; it was not until further *habeas corpus* proceedings had been instituted in the High Court, in the course of which the judge condemned the authorities in the strongest terms for acting "with scant regard for the law and the liberty of the subject", that Mr. Close was actually released.[23] Even when Mr. Close later answered to his bail, he was detained at the close of the day's proceedings and his solicitor denied access to him until his release just before midnight; the remaining charge against him was finally discharged for want of evidence by direction of the trial judge.[24]

The net effect of the stand taken by the judges on the common law rights of accused persons has thus been a good deal less significant than might be assumed. Some small benefits may have been conferred on those concerned, for instance by the decision that the common law rules of natural justice required that all interned persons appearing before the advisory committee set up under the Special Powers Act be provided with a written summary of the information on which suspicion against them is based, and also that they might be represented by a lawyer if they so wished.[25] But even in this respect the court felt obliged to make an exception in any case where the disclosure of the relevant information would be contrary to public safety either by prejudicing the work of the security forces or by revealing their intelligence system. Similarly in the confession cases the courts have been careful to emphasise that it is not for them to interfere with the processes of interrogation. The strict application of the common law rules on arrest, on the admissibility of confessions, and on natural justice may have salved the conscience of the judges in matters of this kind. But it has not generally made any great practical difference to the treatment of individual suspects, given the absolute power vested in the authorities by the Special Powers Act to detain any person they please. The general effect on public confidence in the judicial system of the continual superimposition of 'executive justice' by the security forces when the decisions of the courts have displeased them can scarcely be overestimated.

**Civil actions against the authorities**

A second line of attack in the attempt to use legal means to prevent misconduct by the security forces has been the institution of direct actions for damages against the individual soldiers or policemen alleged to have acted unlawfully or against the authority responsible for their conduct. The eventual outcome in many of these civil actions has been reasonably satisfactory. But once again the response of the authorities has often been such as to offset the beneficial effect which a rapid settlement of such claims might have had.

In the first place the authorities have frequently given the appearance of using every means at their disposal to discourage the initiation of proceedings, and the cases have usually been strenuously contested. In a widely publicised test case arising out of the alleged ill-treatment of those arrested and detained on 9 August 1971 the authorities first sought to block the proceedings by objecting to the discovery of information necessary to the plaintiff's case, and to the admission of evidence by affidavit on his behalf. When it was replied that the plaintiff had gone to live in the Republic for fear of being rearrested, they refused to give any undertaking that if the plaintiff did appear in person he would be given a safe conduct. Eventually after a protracted series of preliminary hearings the county court judge agreed to admit the affidavits, and made the following comment:

> In the absence of explanation or evidence from the defendants [I] make the *prima facie* inference that the Defendants are relying on the plaintiff's fear as a tactic to postpone the hearing of this claim and that *prima facie* they do not *bona fide* desire production of the plaintiff for cross-examination.

After a lengthy trial the judge found for the plaintiff in his action for assault, trespass or battery of the person and awarded him £300 damages, the maximum figure which he could legally give. In the course of his judgment he made further remarks which are indicative of the attitude of the authorities at the time:

> There is a deafening silence from the RUC (generally), and anybody of Army rank higher than Lieutenant Barton (who admits that he is the Senior Officer referred to in paragraph 152 of the Compton Report) as to what went on in the huts, and how and why the procedures which admittedly did develop there were allowed to do so, and why the circumstances in which the men were kept were so primitive notwithstanding the duty of the defendants under the regulations. The urgency of the decision to arrest may be a reason but not a justification. I take the view that the very primitive circumstances must have been foreseen by commanders of greater seniority than Lieutenant Barton,

> that the entire pattern . . . was one of authority, rigid discipline and regimentation . . . and was preconceived. . . . This course was adopted irrespective of whether the people were guilty or innocent, or the relative gravity of matter available in each case to create suspicion.[26]

There can be little doubt that the attitude of the authorities in cases such as this has gone far beyond legitimate defence tactics in an adversary system, and has given support to the belief that the security forces are anxious to deter or prevent the initiation of proceedings against them whenever possible.

Second, there is the question of delay. In the aftermath of the arms searches and curfew in the Lower Falls area early in July 1970 the Army made a point of asking those who had suffered material damage to their houses to seek compensation through official channels. But it was not until 1 December that a test case came before the Belfast Recorder's Court, on what was reported to be the first occasion in which a compensation order under the Special Powers Act had been made. In a similar test case involving a Mr. Kelly, a student who had been arrested in place of his brother on 9 August 1971, and claimed damages for unlawful detention, it was not until 11 January 1973 that the case was finally disposed of by the award of £400 and costs in the High Court. It was held that while in the circumstances Mr. Kelly's detention could not be held to have been unreasonable, and while he had not suffered any ill treatment or any special distress from being confined with persons of different political views from his own, he had not been properly informed of the grounds for his arrest and was entitled to damages in respect of "arrest in the middle of the night, the vexation and perhaps humiliation of the circumstances of his arrest in the presence of his recently reunited family, the interrogation and frustration and deprivation necessarily involved in prison life, not knowing when or how its term would expire."[27] In another case arising out of a notorious incident in which a housewife's eyes had been put out by the discharge of a rubber bullet through her window at point blank range on 4 November 1971, it was not until 19 March 1973 that the Ministry of Defence, while still denying liability, agreed to pay £35,000 in compensation.

Delays of at least this length are commonplace in civil actions for personal injury. But in cases where misconduct by the security forces is alleged there is a special need for speed if confidence in the availability of legal redress is to be maintained. The figures given by the Attorney-General in April 1973 are indicative of the general lack of urgency on the part of the authorities: of the 150 civil claims against the Crown by those who claimed to have been ill-treated by the security forces, only 39 had been settled by plaintiffs accepting payment.[28] Specially expedited procedures have been introduced to deal with compensation payments for businesses affected by terrorist explosions. It can scarcely be doubted that a similar scheme to ensure the speedy settlement of disputed incidents would be of the greatest assistance in maintaining good relations between the security forces and the local population in troubled areas.

**Criminal prosecution**

The belated satisfaction which may eventually be obtained in a civil action is also offset by the knowledge that no penalty is thereby imposed on those responsible for the unlawful action. This fact, and the desire among some members of the minority community to avenge what appears to them to be the wholly unjustifiable conduct of some soldiers and policemen, has led to calls for criminal charges to be laid in respect of some of the more serious incidents, in particular those in which it has been alleged that persons arrested have been deliberately beaten up in the course of interrogation and those in which it has been alleged that innocent civilians have been deliberately shot by Army patrols. It was revealed by the Attorney-General in April 1973 that there had been demands for criminal prosecution against 37 members of the security forces for inflicting bodily harm and 62 cases of unlawful shooting, malicious damage and larceny.[29]

The legal position in such cases is relatively straightforward. Since members of the security forces are in exactly the same position in law as anyone else, except insofar as special powers of arrest and questioning are conferred on them by the Special Powers Act, any physical injury inflicted by a soldier or policeman deliberately and without lawful justification constitutes a criminal offence. Thus, where the complainant has simply been pushed around, a charge of common assault might be laid; where he has suffered real physical injury, as in cases of alleged beatings, a charge of aggravated assault or malicious or felonious wounding might be laid; and where the victim has been killed or seriously injured by gunfire, a charge of manslaughter, murder, or attempted murder might be laid.

The definition of 'lawful justification' depends largely on the common law conception of what is reasonable in the circumstances and in relation to the complainant's own conduct. Reasonable force may be applied, for instance, to prevent escape from lawful custody or to prevent the commission of a crime. In respect of the use of weapons, these rules are clearly and precisely stated in the yellow card issued to every soldier. This sets out the circumstances in which he may lawfully open fire: for instance "against a person carrying a firearm, but only if you have reason to think that he is about to use it for offensive purposes and he refuses to halt when called upon to do so . . . ", or "if there is no other way to protect yourself or those whom it is your duty to protect from the danger of being killed or seriously injured." Though some changes have been made in the wording on the yellow card from time to time, the validity of the rules contained in it as an accurate statement of the common law rights of the armed forces has not been seriously questioned. Accordingly if it can be shown that in a particular case the rules in the yellow card have not been followed, this would be *prima facie* evidence that an offence had been committed, subject always to the possible defence of reasonable mistake. Allegations that soldiers have not adhered to the rules in the yellow card have frequently been made, for instance in the cases of the shooting of three alleged bank robbers in Newry in October 1971, the civilians shot dead in Derry on 'Bloody Sunday' in January 1972, and those shot dead in the Ardoyne area of Belfast in the spring of 1973. Cases in which admitted members of the IRA have been shot dead, as in the case of Joe McCann in the Markets area in the spring of 1972, raise more difficult issues, but here too it is probably unlawful for soldiers to shoot to kill merely to prevent escape.[30]

Relatively few of the cases in which demands for criminal prosecution against members of the security forces have been made, however, have come before the courts, and, in those which have, the result has seldom proved satisfactory to the complainants. In a number of cases the defendants have been acquitted. In others the cases have not been pursued beyond a certain point. In others it has proved impossible to gain the assistance of the prosecuting authorities, as for instance in the cases arising out of the Bloody Sunday shootings. There is accordingly a widespread belief among members of the minority community that it is futile to attempt to pursue a serious criminal charge against the security forces. The various reasons for this belief and their validity are worth considering in some detail.

First there was the practical difficulty of initiating criminal proceedings, particularly prior to the establishment of the Director of Public Prosecutions in 1972. In theory there was nothing to prevent ordinary individuals from exercising their common law right to initiate private prosecutions. But in practice this was not as simple as it sounds. One problem in cases involving the security forces was the identification of the particular policemen or soldiers involved. In coroner's courts the military and police witnesses are (for obvious security reasons) identified only by a letter. Another problem is that coroner's courts in Northern Ireland cannot bring in any verdict which implies that a criminal offence was involved in the death. This restriction, introduced in the 1950's, effectively prevents a coroner or his jury from putting pressure on the authorities to initiate criminal proceedings by entering a verdict of murder or manslaughter where that appears, *prima facie,* to be a justifiable inference. Some of these difficulties could have been surmounted by the effective use of such standard legal procedures as an application for discovery of the identity of a particular solider. But no private prosecution was in fact initiated. It was not until the new office of Director of Public Prosecutions was set up, with the express duty of looking into cases referred by private individuals, that any serious criminal charges were laid against members of the security forces.

Second, there is the problem of collecting evidence. Again it is theoretically possible for a private individual or lawyer to undertake this. But in cases where the Army is involved and ballistic evidence is required, official cooperation is a practical necessity. In any event, there has been a tendency for complainants to expect any necessary investigation to be carried out for them by the police. There have then been complaints that inquiries have not been pursued by the police with sufficient vigour, allegedly with the ulterior motive of preventing any proceedings being started. Some of this apparent lack of vigour, however, is due to the insistence of the army that questioning of army personnel should be carried out by the military police. Quite apart from the appearance of partiality which this rule creates, the division of an investigation between civilian and military police is not calculated to increase its efficacy. More seriously, there have been allegations that witnesses of some of the more serious shooting incidents have been deliberately harassed and even shot at by soldiers to deter them from giving evidence which might lead to conviction, as in the case of a civilian shot dead by the Paratroop Regiment in the Ardoyne area in April 1973. Finally, there is the natural tendency of soldiers and policemen to seek to cover up any misconduct by their colleagues.

The results in those few cases which have come to court since the Director of Public Prosecutions has taken charge bear out some of these complaints and allegations. In a case heard in October 1972 involving charges of assault against two police constables and two soldiers, in which the jury brought verdicts of simple assault against the soldiers only, the judge made the following comments:

> I find this case unsatisfactory in the way it was presented to the court. It is a matter of great importance, and it is clear that Hughes was assaulted very badly while he was in the custody of the security forces. It is clear that this court has not heard anything like the truth about the matter. I am satisfied that there has been a conspiracy of silence on the part of some people, and I am directing that the papers be sent to the Attorney-General.[31]

Similar problems arose in a case against two detectives and a soldier alleged to have beaten up three men arrested and interrogated in Belfast in April 1972. It was clear from the medical evidence that someone must have given the complainants a severe beating, and the defence case was that the men must have been beaten by unknown army personnel before being presented for questioning. In the event the judge directed that the case against the soldiers should be dismissed, and the two detectives were found not guilty by the jury.[32] Some cases have resulted in convictions. It was reported in May 1973 that since December 1970 29 soldiers had been tried for offences against civilians: 14 out of 25 had been convicted of simple assault but only one out of four of the more serious offence of wounding.[33] It is clear from our study of reported cases that most convictions have been for minor off-duty offences, such as public house brawls. The more serious charge of unlawful violence by soldiers on duty or by those conducting interrogations have almost without exception proved unsuccessful.

A final difficulty of a rather different kind is the possible existence of a political veto on proceedings against the security forces. It has been admitted that the results of police and army investigations of criminal complaints are sent first to the Northern Ireland Office before being forwarded to the Director of Public Prosecutions. There have been specific allegations, which have not been satisfactorily answered, that possible proceedings over some of the Bloody Sunday shootings were blocked by a directive from the Attorney-General. It is impossible to resolve this issue on the evidence available. But it cannot be doubted that the Director does lack the absolute independence of government which was originally recommended in the Hunt and MacDermott reports. (Below p. 44)

It is clearly difficult to come to any firm conclusion on the general issue of criminal proceedings against the security forces. The troops are operating under incredibly difficult conditions, and it may be argued that they should not be open to the additional hazard of criminal liability for occasional breaches of discipline. On the other hand it is inconsistent for the authorities to stress the need to maintain the ordinary law if the security forces are to be granted effective immunity. It may be that the dilemma would be better resolved, as in the case of civil proceedings for damages, by the establishment of a special security tribunal to hear both compensatory and disciplinary actions involving the security forces. But it cannot seriously be contended that the present system inspires the kind of public confidence in the impartiality of the judicial system which is so necessary in Northern Ireland.

**International proceedings**

Brief mention should also be made of the various attempts to seek redress against alleged misconduct by the security forces through the European Commission on Human Rights. The first applications to the Commission were made by Bernadette Devlin in 1969 in respect of her conviction for incitement to riot in Derry, and by the Campaign for Social Justice in 1971 in respect of housing discrimination in Dungannon. Cases have also been raised in respect of alleged torture or ill treatment of those detained and interrogated and in respect of the Bloody Sunday shootings. Without going into the details of the procedure adopted by the Commission two comments may perhaps be made. First, the provisions for representation at the Commission are inadequate. Continual problems have arisen over the various American attorneys who have undertaken to pursue the Northern Ireland cases in Strasbourg, but have for one reason or another had to withdraw. Secondly there is the ever-present issue of delay. Proceedings in these cases drag on interminably. If the European Commission is to act as an effective aid to individuals as well as a form of political pressure on member governments its procedures will have to be considerably streamlined.

## REFERENCES


1. For the use of the Act prior to 1936 see *Report of a Commission of Inquiry appointed to examine the purpose and effect of the Civil Authorities (Special Powers) Acts (Northern Ireland) 1922 & 1933,* National Council for Civil Liberties, 1936.
2. *R. v Governor of Belfast Prison, ex parte O'Hanlon,*(1922) 56 I.L.T.R. 170.
3. Vol. 17, *sub tit.* Northern Ireland 1950.
4. *Report of the Commission to consider legal procedures to deal with terrorist activities in Northern Ireland,* Cmnd. 5185, 1972, para. 32.
5. For further details see 'The Evolution, Disintegration and Possible Reconstruction of the Northern Ireland Constitution' by Claire Palley, *Anglo-American Law Review,* Vol. 1, 1972, p. 413.
6. Cmd. 532, Belfast.
7. Cmd. 566, Belfast.
8. Cmnd. 4823.
9. H.C. 220, April 1972.

10. Cmnd. 4901, March 1972.
11. Cmnd. 5185.
12. See *Justice Denied* by Samual Dash, National Council for Civil Liberties, 1972.
13. H.C. 220, para. 85.
14. *The Times,* 2 September 1971.
15. *In re Keenan & Another* [1971] 3 W.L.R. 844.
16. *R. v JPs for the County of the City of Londonderry, ex parte Hume & Others,* 23 February, 1972.
17. *In re McElduff,* 12 October 1971.
18. *Kelly v. Minister of Home Affairs,* 11 January 1972.
19. *R. v Meehan,* January 1973.
20. *R. v Gargan,* 10 May 1972.
21. *R. v Flynn & Leonard,* 24 May 1972.
22. 855 H.C. Deb., col. 388, 17 April 1973.
23. *In re Close,* 22 December 1971.
24. 'The Rule of Law in Northern Ireland' by Tom Hadden, *New Law Journal,* 17 February 1972, p. 161.
25. *In re Mackey,* 16 December 1971.
26. *Moore v Shillington and Minister of Defence,* Armagh County Court, 3 January and 18 February 1972.
27. *Kelly v Faulkner,* 11 January 1973.
28. 855 H.C. Deb., Col. 388, 17 April 1973.
29. 855 H.C. Deb., Col. 388, 17 April 1973.
30. For a more detailed discussion see 'The Myths of Martial Law' by Tom Hadden, *Fortnight,* 29 October 1971.
31. *Irish Times,* 18-19 October 1972.
32. *Irish News,* 14-17 March 1973.
33. 856 H.C. Deb., Written Answers, Col 201, 11 May 1973.

## CHAPTER V

# The Courts in Emergency Conditions

The Westminster government has laid great stress on the desirability of relying on the ordinary courts in dealing with the developing emergency in Northern Ireland. Even after the introduction of internment without trial in August 1971, the authorities have emphasised their intention of using the ordinary court whenever possible. Mr. Whitelaw, in opening the Second Reading of the Northern Ireland (Emergency Provisions) Bill stated: "We will continue to bring suspected persons before the courts wherever possible". This approach is frequently justified by the publication of statistics on the number of persons being brought before the courts for terrorist offences. And one of the reasons given for retaining detention without trial in the proposed Bill has been the notion that only in that way can interference with the ordinary courts be avoided:

> It has been argued that detention could be ended if the ordinary criminal procedures were changed even more radically than was recommended by the Diplock Commission. The Commission itself considered this problem. Its conclusion was that it would be far too dangerous to alter the administration of justice by removing safeguards which it considered fundamental to the criminal process in normal times. Its reason was that the reputation of the courts and trust in them would suffer and might not recover.[1]

The main drawback with this policy is that it overlooks the general lack of confidence among the minority community in the administration of justice. There can be no doubt about this. Public statements on the subject have been made by all sections of the Roman Catholic community. In May 1971 the leaders of the main opposition party in the Stormont Parliament put down two motions, one calling for the removal from office of the Recorder of Belfast and the other censuring the Attorney-General, both on the grounds of political bias in the administration of justice. In April 1971 a group of Roman Catholic priests refused to fill in their census forms as a protest against alleged discrimination in the courts. Father Faul, a Roman Catholic priest in Dungannon who has published a number of statements on judicial matters, put it this way: "Our people are afraid of the courts; they believe the judicial system as it operates in the blatantly sectarian conditions of life here is loaded against them".[2] Later in the same year, after the introduction of internment without trial, a group of prominent Roman Catholics made a comprehensive attack on the administration of justice:

> Criminal charges are preferred much more forcefully against Catholics than against any other section of the population, both in selecting the number and nature of the charges to be brought, in the seriousness or otherwise of the Act under which the charges are brought, the method of commencement of the charges (whether by arrest or by service of summons), in determining whether bail should be opposed and in collecting, selecting and presenting evidence to the courts.[3]

Concern over the administration of justice has not been restricted to representatives of the Roman Catholic Community in Northern Ireland. In May 1971 more than one hundred solicitors and barristers from both communities called on the Law Society and the Bar Council to set up an inquiry as a matter of urgency into the administration of the criminal law. More recently an *Irish Times* editorial made the following comment on the partiality with which internment without trial was operated:

> To the minority the great inconsistency is the feeling that while Long Kesh still holds about 250 men, there are others freely walking the streets of Belfast, appearing on television, issuing statements to the press, who have objectives quite as inflammatory as those of the Provisionals and arms to back them. On one side a man may find himself behind wire for, perhaps, little more than the possession of a Gaelic grammar, a membership card in the GAA (Gaelic Athletic Association) the reasoning goes; on the other side, it appears to them, anything goes.[4]

In the light of this evidence of widespread lack of confidence it is difficult to share the complacency of the authorities.

**Specific allegations**

This general concern over the administration of justice covers all the various stages of the judicial process. From the choice of charges and the decision on bail to conviction and sentence, Some of the specific allegations are as follows.

On the choice of charge the main complaint has been that Roman Catholics have been charged with more serious offences than Protestants for broadly similar behaviour. Allegations of this kind were especially prevalent following the enactment of the Criminal Justice (Temporary Provisions) Act (Northern Ireland) 1970. This made a six month prison sentence mandatory for a long list of public order offences including riotous and disorderly behaviour. The statute was soon amended to exclude disorderly behaviour when it was found that a number of persons who had been involved in domestic disputes and charged with disorderly behaviour were falling under the mandatory six month sentence. But the amendment created an obvious means by which the police could determine the length of sentence to be imposed on defendants, and it was not long before allegations were made that Roman Catholics were being charged with riotous behaviour and Protestants with disorderly behaviour for similar conduct. In February 1971, for example, two bands of women assembled outside the Belfast Magistrates Court. One group were Roman Catholics, protesting against the prosecution of a man charged with wearing an IRA uniform at a funeral. Trouble broke out between these women and a group of Protestant counter-protestors; 40 Roman Catholics were arrested and many charged with riotous behaviour. No Protestants were arrested. Six weeks later some 2,000 Loyalists attempted to storm a Roman Catholic church in East Belfast. Only thirteen persons were arrested and only three were charged with riotous behaviour.

Allegations have also been made that the police have deliberately acted in such a way as to determine sentence in a different and more subtle situation. The

Special Powers Act prescribes sentences for certain offences, but the minimum sentences are considerably heavier if the offences are tried on indictment than if they are tried summarily. In addition the Magistrates Courts Act (Northern Ireland) 1956 provides that certain charges not dealt with within six months of the offence must be tried on indictment. Thus by delaying proceedings for six months it was possible to ensure that persons charged with certain offences received a lengthy sentence. It has been alleged that the police purposely delayed bringing a charge of collecting police car numbers – an offence under the Special Powers Act – against a Mr. Cosgrove for this reason. When the case came before the court on indictment the judge had no option but to impose the minimum sentence of three years imprisonment.[5]

In respect of decisions on bail it has been alleged that Protestants are more likely than Roman Catholics to be granted bail for similar offences. In 1970 a number of opposition MPs walked out of the Stormont Parliament following what they regarded as an unsatisfactory reply to a question about two apparently inconsistent bail decisions. In one case a Protestant charged with possessing a number of firearms was granted bail; in another a Roman Catholic charged with having a rusty firearm was remanded in custody. Members of the judiciary have publicly declared their concern over bail decisions. In January 1973 two County Court judges complained about lack of uniformity in bail decisions.[6] Soon after a Resident Magistrate suggested that it was high time that the authorities formulated some policy on the granting of bail as a guide to the courts.[7]

Finally, there have been frequent criticisms of decisions on conviction and sentence in particular cases. It has been suggested that in riot cases magistrates have been far too ready to accept the evidence of the security forces without question, and that Roman Catholics are more likely to be convicted than Protestants. Some defending solicitors have even said that there are certain types of case in which it is pointless to attempt to secure acquittal. On sentencing, comparisons of cases in which Roman Catholics have apparently been dealt with more severely than Protestants are often made. In 1970 there was a public outcry when a Roman Catholic received a six month sentence for writing 'no tea here' on a wall; this was compared with a case only a week later in which a former member of the B Specials received a suspended sentence of twelve months on four charges of unlawfully supplying guns. Again in April 1971 there was widespread concern at a case in which a Roman Catholic received a twelve month jail sentence for shouting 'Up the IRA' on the fringes of a Protestant procession.

All these allegations have received wide publicity in the local press, particularly in the *Irish News,* the main organ of the Roman Catholic community in Northern Ireland. There can be no doubt that the result has been to strengthen the longstanding distrust of the court system of the part of many Roman Catholics, and to reinforce their view that the whole of the security operation has been geared primarily to the suppression of Republican activity rather than to the impartial maintenance of law and order in Loyalist and Republican areas alike. The frequent references by both Unionist and British politicians to their successes in dealing with disorder and terrorism by judicial means have been interpreted as little more than a propaganda exercise to conceal the basic bias in the system.

**An independent prosecutor**

In the early stages of the civil rights campaign the question of public confidence in the judicial process was treated seriously. The report of the Hunt Committee on the reorganisation of the Royal Ulster Constabulary recognised that "the impartiality of the police may be questioned if they are responsible for deciding who shall be prosecuted and thereafter acting as prosecutor" and recommended the establishment of a system of independent public prosecutors on the Scottish model.[8] This recommendation was given further and more detailed consideration by the MacDermott Committee,[9] and eventually resulted in the creation of a new office of Director of Public Prosecutions for Northern Ireland with full responsibility for the selection and prosecution of all serious criminal charges and for advising the courts on bail applications throughout Northern Ireland. The first Director was appointed early in 1972, and has progressively taken control of the situation. All cases tried on indictment, and all summary charges which have any direct or indirect connection with public disorder or terrorist activities, are now dealt with by the Director's staff. Many less serious cases, especially motoring offences, are still dealt with exclusively by the police. The Director is generally independent, but remains responsible to the Attorney-General of Northern Ireland for the due performance of his functions, a fact which has raised some doubts as to the impartiality of decisions in relation to the prosecution of members of the security forces.

Apart from this, the response of the authorities to allegations of bias in the judicial system has been to emphasise the total impartiality of the judiciary, and to imply that anyone who criticises the courts is a politically motivated propagandist. It is the purpose of this chapter to investigate the validity of this response.

**The problem of assessment**

It is clearly presumptuous for any commentator or researcher to place his own judgment above that of a court of law. There is no absolute criterion of truth or justice to fall back on. Questions of guilt or innocence and of the correctness of a particular decision on bail or on sentence are not amenable to objective or scientific analysis.

All these problems are particularly acute in Northern Ireland, given the power of rumour and the readiness of members of both communities to believe or persuade themselves of virtually anything. But in view of the fundamental importance of the issues raised it would be wrong to refuse to attempt an assessment on the ground that certainty cannot be attained. We have therefore decided to accept some imperfections in research methodology and to make the best of the material and resources available to us. We set out our methods and the nature of the material so that readers may make their own assessment.

In respect of decisions at the lower court level we have relied on an observational study of selected magistrates courts during the spring and summer of 1972. This was carried out with the assistance of small grants from both the Cobden Trust and the Legal Research Committee of the Law Faculty at Queen's University. Nine courts were covered: the Custody and Summons Courts in Belfast, which sit daily, and the periodic sittings at Coleraine, Limavady, Londonderry, Lisburn, Lurgan, Portadown and Newtownbreda. All of these are presided over by a single stipendiary magistrate. Teams of two observers drawn from the Queen's University Law Faculty and the Social Administration Department at the New University of Ulster sat in on cases heard from the end of March until the second week in April, and from the middle of June to the end of the first week in July. The first period covered a number of cases arising out of the Loyalist strikes and protests called in response to the imposition of direct rule in March 1972; there was nothing corresponding to this in the second period, but there were a number of cases in both periods arising out of the sporadic disorders which have continued over the whole period in Roman Catholic areas.

Each pair of observers, generally one Protestant and one Roman Catholic student, was instructed to make two independent records on prepared schedules of all that happened in court in each case heard, and in particular of applications for bail or legal aid and decisions on conviction and sentence. Though the observers were generally permitted to use the press box, they were not given access to any court records or files, and were thus in the same position as any other member of the public or press. On the basis of what they observed, the teams were also asked to draw attention to any notable features of particular cases or of the court's procedure in general, and to comment on what appeared to them to be strange or doubtful decisions. They were also instructed to note the apparent religion of the defendants (where that was revealed in the course of the proceedings), their social class and their demeanor in court. On all these points each observer was instructed to make his own assessment independently, and to discuss the matter with his colleague in any case of doubt or conflict.

In all 568 cases were covered in the survey. These were later classified into four broad categories: (i) offences which could be considered to have 'political' connotations, in the sense of being in some way connected with the 'troubles'; (ii) 'ordinary' criminal offences against property; (iii) motoring offences; and (iv) miscellaneous offences Fuller details of this classification and the distribution of cases are set out in Table I in the Appendix. The number of cases in each category heard in each court are similarly listed in Table II.

This material has been used in two ways. In respect of the simpler details recorded for almost all cases a limited amount of quantified analysis has been possible, for example in relation to differences in treatment of Protestant and

Roman Catholic defendants in 'political' and 'non-political' cases. Where quantification has not been possible, because of the subjective nature of the observers' comments or the lack of detail in some reports, the material has been used in a more discursive manner, for instance in contrasting the treatment of two apparently similar cases. The dangers of this type of analysis are obvious, but in relation to the broad issue of public confidence with which we are concerned, it does have the advantage of highlighting those aspects of individual decisions which are perhaps most likely to affect public opinion in general.

For higher court decisions it has not been possible to organise a survey of the same kind as for the magistrates courts, because of the very much longer time taken by each case.[10] Instead we have relied on a study of all cases heard at the Belfast City Commission in the period from January to June 1973, when a large number of cases involving both Loyalist and Republican defendants came to trial. The primary source for this was the official court records, but additional details, notably the apparent religion of the defendant, were obtained from the Crown depositions. In all the study covered over 1,250 counts against 334 defendants of which 159 were identified as Protestants and 158 as Roman Catholics. A detailed classification of the cases is set out in Table VI of the Appendix.

As in the magistrates court study there is no question of reaching any final conclusion on the impartiality of the courts on the basis of this material. But it has permitted some assessment of their performance in dealing with cases against defendants from both communities in what appear from the records to have been similar cases. We have also compared the results with a prior survey of cases reported in the *Belfast Telegraph* over the same period. Since the public must rely on newspapers in making its own assessment this comparison is clearly significant.

In the sections which follow, each of the main aspects of judicial decision-making in both magistrates and higher courts will be dealt with in turn, beginning with the preliminary decisions on bail and legal aid, and progressing through the selection of charges, conviction or acquittal, and sentencing. Where appropriate, use has also been made of other facts and figures from Parliamentary sources and the press.

**Bail/custody decisions**

One of the most frequent allegations against the magistrates courts has been of the discriminatory practice of remanding Roman Catholic defendants in custody while in similar cases Protestant defendants are remanded on bail. Our observers were instructed to record all cases in which the question of bail was raised and to note the attitude taken by the police in such cases.

In all, 114 relevant bail/custody decisions were observed. The majority of these, as is shown by the figures in Table 5.1, were made in hearings involving 'political' offences, and as might be expected most of the remands in custody were in respect of these cases. Thus bail was granted in only 16% of the 74 offences, as opposed to 78% of other offences in which the nature of the charges was revealed in court. The fact that bail was granted in only 10% of the cases in which details of the charge were not revealed suggests that most of these were also of a 'political' character.

**Table 5.1. Number of defendants granted bail or remanded in custody Magistrates Courts Survey 1972**

| *Offence Category* | | | *Bail* | *Remand in custody* |
|---|---|---|---|---|
| A. | Political: | | | |
| | 1. | Rioting | 1 | — |
| | 2. | Firearms | 11 | 40 |
| | 3. | Explosives | — | 11 |
| | 4. | Against the person | — | 10 |
| | 5. | Other | — | 1 |
| | **Total** | | **12** | **62** |
| B. | Motoring: | | No Bail/Remand decisions | |
| C. | Property: | | | |
| | 1. | Shoplifting | — | — |
| | 2. | Burglary | 2 | 2 |
| | 3. | Other theft | 4 | 1 |
| | 4. | Fraud, etc. | 1 | 1 |
| | **Total** | | **7** | **4** |
| D. | Miscellaneous: | | | |
| | 1. | Against the person | 4 | 1 |
| | 2. | Disorderly behaviour | — | — |
| | 3. | Other specified | 3 | 1 |
| | 4. | Other unspecified | 2 | 18 |
| | **Total** | | **9** | **20** |
| | **GRAND TOTAL** | | **28** | **86** |

Within the categories of 'political' and 'non-political' offences, Roman Catholics and Protestants were treated differently as shown in Table 5.2. The situation here is complicated by the fact that a number of defendants on political charges refused to recognise the court, and were thus procedurally barred from applying for bail. It may be assumed that the vast majority of such defendants were Roman Catholics in view of the IRA tradition of refusing to recognise the legitimacy of Northern Ireland Courts, though recently some Loyalists have also refused to recognise courts on different grounds. But even if these cases are ignored, there was a substantial difference in the treatment of Protestants and Roman Catholics charged with political offences: only one in five (21%) of Roman Catholics were granted bail compared with almost half (46%) of the Protestants. In respect of non-political offences, however, there is no such difference, with roughly half of all defendants, except those refusing to recognise the court, being granted bail.

It does not necessarily follow that this substantial difference in the treatment of Roman Catholics and Protestants charged with political offences is due to unjustified discrimination by magistrates. When the cases were matched on a number of criteria it appeared that the Roman Catholics in our sample had generally been charged with more serious offences than Protestants. This does not in itself refute the allegations of bias, in view of the apparent bias in the selection of charges discussed below.

Table 5.2. **Number and proportion of defendants granted bail shown by type of offence and religion. Magistrates Courts Survey 1972**

| | *Bail granted* | | *Bail refused* | | *Total* | |
|---|---|---|---|---|---|---|
| | No | % | No | % | No | % |
| **Political offences** | | | | | | |
| Does not recognise the court | – | – | 31 | 100 | 31 | 100 |
| Catholic | 6 | 21 | 22 | 79 | 28 | 100 |
| Protestant | 6 | 46 | 7 | 54 | 13 | 100 |
| Religion not known | – | – | 2 | 100 | 2 | 100 |
| **Total** | **12** | **16** | **62** | **84** | **74** | **100** |
| **Other offences** | | | | | | |
| Does not recognise the court | – | – | 7 | 100 | 7 | 100 |
| Catholic | 6 | 50 | 6 | 50 | 12 | 100 |
| Protestant | 8 | 47 | 9 | 53 | 17 | 100 |
| Religion not known | 2 | 50 | 2 | 50 | 4 | 100 |
| **Total** | **16** | **40** | **24** | **60** | **40** | **100** |

The explanation for this may well lie in the attitude of the police, who play an important part in bail/custody decisions. It is customary for magistrates to ask the police for their view on the granting of bail, and they are often reluctant to overrule police objections. This has been one of the major complaints about current practice in the granting and refusal of bail in England, as revealed in a recent Cobden Trust publication.[11] The results of the current survey raises similar doubts about the role of the police in Northern Ireland. It should be noted, however, that the task of advising the courts on bail decisions is now formally the responsibility of the Director of Public Prosecutions, though at the time of the survey this function had not yet been effectively undertaken.

Bail was discussed in open court in 55 (48%) of the cases covered in the survey. The police expressed a view in almost all (87%) of these. The nature of the police advice in cases involving Roman Catholics and Protestants is set out in Table 5.3

Table 5.3. **Number of bail/custody decisions by type of offence, police view and religion. Magistrates Courts Survey 1972**

| | | *Bail granted* | | *Bail refused* | | *Total* | |
|---|---|---|---|---|---|---|---|
| | | No | % | No | % | No | % |
| **Political offences:** | | | | | | | |
| Police objections | (Catholic | 4 | 21 | 15 | 79 | 19 | 100 |
| | (Protestant | 2 | 34 | 4 | 66 | 6 | 100 |
| | (Not known | – | – | – | – | – | – |
| No Police objections | (Catholic | 1 | 100 | – | – | 1 | 100 |
| | (Protestant | 2 | 50 | 2 | 50 | 4 | 100 |
| | (Not known | – | – | – | – | – | – |
| | **Total** | **9** | **30** | **21** | **70** | **30** | **100** |
| **Non-Political offences:** | | | | | | | |
| Police objections | (Catholic | – | – | 1 | 100 | 1 | 100 |
| | (Protestant | – | – | 1 | 100 | 1 | 100 |
| | (Not known | – | – | 1 | 100 | 1 | 100 |
| No Police objections | (Catholic | 5 | 100 | – | – | 5 | 100 |
| | (Protestant | 6 | 86 | 1 | 14 | 7 | 100 |
| | (Not known | 2 | 67 | 1 | 33 | 3 | 100 |
| | **Total** | **13** | **72** | **5** | **28** | **18** | **100** |

The figures show a clear bias in police attitudes: in political cases they objected to bail in 95% of cases involving Roman Catholics, compared with only 60% of cases involving Protestants. While some of this difference may again be explained by the greater seriousness of the charges against Roman Catholics in the sample, the case reports showed that the police frequently argued that Roman Catholics were less likely than Protestants to answer bail. Two reasons were given for this: first that Roman Catholics were more likely to evade the jurisdiction of the court by fleeing over the border, an option supposedly not open to Protestants; and secondly that it may be more difficult and dangerous for the security force to rearrest in a Roman Catholic area than in a Protestant one if the need should arise. There may be some justification for these views. Figures produced in answer to a Parliamentary question showed that over a period of a year 69 persons had absconded while on bail.[12] But they do reveal a clear sectarian bias in the thinking of the police on this issue. It should be noted, however, that the magistrates did go some way to correct such bias in 'political' charges by refusing bail to two of the four Protestants in whose cases no police objection was raised, and by granting bail to four of the nineteen Roman Catholics in the face of police objections.

Nonetheless there were cases in the study which appeared to show a bias in the final decision by the magistrates. There were, for example, two cases in which Protestant defendants who were charged with firearms offences received bail. In the first case a Protestant was charged with the possession of 57 rounds of .22 ammunition; legal aid was applied for on the grounds that this was a serious offence; later bail was also applied for; there were no police objections and bail was granted on £500 recognisances with two sureties. In the second case another Protestant was accused of possessing a firearm and ammunition; the defence claimed there was no political motive; the magistrate did not question this submission and granted bail on £100 recognisances with two sureties. In neither of these two cases was it apparent why bail should have been granted for what were admittedly serious offences for which Roman Catholics defendants are uniformly remanded in custody. Cases such as these may clearly be used, and have in fact been used, in support of allegations that the courts are blatantly partial in accepting that it is much less serious for Protestants to be caught in illegal possession of firearms ("for self defence") than Roman Catholics (who are assumed to be terrorists).

Further support for this view was obtained in the Belfast City Commission survey. Of the total number of 334 defendants just under half (45%) had been remanded on bail. But proportionately more Protestants (59%) than Roman Catholics (27%) had been granted bail. This was partly attributable to the less serious nature of the charges against Protestant defendants in firearms cases, as discussed below. The difference could be further justified by the fact that a higher proportion of Roman Catholics who had been released on bail did not appear to answer the charges against them. But the figures do give prima facie backing to complaints about discriminatory treatment.

Table 5.4 **The number of defendants remanded on bail and in custody in cases cases for trial at the Belfast City Commission, January - June 1973.**

| | *Bail* | | *Custody* | | *No details* | | *Total* | |
|---|---|---|---|---|---|---|---|---|
| | No | % | No | % | No | % | No | % |
| Protestants | 94 | 59 | 64 | 40 | 1 | 1 | 159 | 100 |
| Roman Catholics | 43 | 27 | 113 | 72 | 2 | 2 | 158 | 100 |
| Religion unknown | 12 | 71 | 5 | 29 | - | - | 17 | 100 |
| **Total** | **149** | **45** | **182** | **54** | **3** | **1** | **334** | **100** |

It is difficult to reach any firm conclusion on this evidence as to the validity of the general complaints over the granting and refusal of bail, given the lack of detail on the precise nature of the conduct alleged against those concerned in many of the cases. But the figures do suggest that there is some ground for concern over the attitudes of the police in this matter, and also that magistrates do not always make sufficient inquiry into the grounds for police objections. Any person remanded in custody has the right to appeal to a High Court judge, and in a number of cases bail has been ordered. Nonetheless the lack of precision in current practice in this area does make it easy for plausible grounds for complaint to be raised. The duty of maintaining general supervision over the bail/custody decision has now been entrusted to the Director of Public Prosecutions, as noted above. If public confidence in the impartiality of his advice to magistrates, and in the impartiality of the magistrates' ultimate decisions is to be increased, it would be desirable for the Director to institute a uniform procedure for dealing with bail applications, and for the magistrates to state clearly and precisely the grounds on which their decisions are based.[13]

**Legal aid and legal representation**

It is clearly in the interests of justice that persons facing serious charges and those who may be remanded in custody should have the advice of a qualified lawyer in the presentation of their case. In Northern Ireland as in Britain those who are not able to afford legal representation from their own resources are entitled to apply for legal aid. The findings of the magistrates court study on this aspect of the judicial system indicate that there is little cause for concern insofar as criminal cases are concerned. In 67% of the total of 568 cases, as shown by the detailed analysis in Table IV of the Appendix, the defendant was legally represented, and representation was clearly more frequent in the more serious cases. In the political offences, apart from the 38 cases in which the defendants refused to recognise the court and thus did not permit themselves to be represented, all defendants were represented. Defendants who recognised the court were represented in 75 of the 76 bail/custody decisions.

These findings were similar to those of a prior study of the operation of the legal aid system in summary trials in Belfast in June 1971, in which it was found that 73% of all defendants were legally represented.[14] This study also showed that relatively few applications for legal aid were refused. This is borne out by the official figures for 1970–71 and 1971–72, set out in Table V of the Appendix, which showed a refusal rate of only 3%.[15] The rate of refusal for similar applications in England is very much higher. There would not seem to be any cause for concern over the operation of the legal aid system in criminal cases in Northern Ireland.

**Selection of charges**

Prior to the establishment of the office of the Director of Public Prosecutions in 1972 the decisions on whether to prosecute and what charges to prefer were made by the police and their legal advisers. Now the Director of Public Prosecutions is formally responsible for the prosecution of indictable offences and such classes of summary offences as he thinks should be conducted by him. Our study of the work of the magistrates courts was conducted during the period of transition when some classes of summary offences later taken over by the Director were still being dealt with by the police.

Though full details of the circumstances relevant to the selection of charges were not available to us, the study did suggest that there had been a degree of discrimination in the cases covered. This was particularly apparent in cases of riotous and disorderly behaviour. During the study 21 cases of disorderly behaviour were observed. In eleven of these the defendant was identified as a Roman Catholic and in eight as a Protestant. In every one of the 13 cases of riotous behaviour the defendant was identified as a Roman Catholic. The cases of disorderly behaviour were then examined more closely to see if the circumstances justified this apparent difference in treatment of Roman Catholic and Protestant defendants. In at least three of the cases the circumstances, insofar as they were revealed in open court, would appear to have warranted a charge of riotous behaviour. In all of these the defendant was identified as a Protestant. In one of the cases a Protestant was in a crowd of young people throwing stones at the Army from behind a UDA barricade; the Resident Magistrate commented that there was nothing political in the case, though it was a serious offence; he was taking a lenient view and would fine the accused £30. In another of the cases a 19-year old Protestant girl was charged with disorderly behaviour after being arrested from a crowd which was stoning troops in the Shankhill Road. In the third case two rival crowds were stoning each other; a Protestant man was said by the police to have been encouraging one crowd to engage in hostilities with the other. Cases such as these raise suspicions that an element of bias, whether deliberate or unconscious, has entered into the selection of charges.

There were in addition a number of cases in which the Magistrates themselves expressed their concern over the selection of the charges. In two cases in which the defendant had been charged with riotous behaviour, it was clear that in the Magistrate's view an incorrect charge had been laid. In one the Magistrate remarked that he would have preferred to convict the defendant on a charge of common assault. In the other he suggested that a charge of assault would have been more appropriate.

The possibility of bias was examined in respect of the 'non-political' offences. No evidence of sectarian discrimination was found, but in some cases the selection of charges appeared to have been somewhat arbitrary. It was particularly difficult to understand the rationale behind the choice between charges of careless and dangerous driving. There were a number of 'pairs' of cases in which in similar circumstances one defendant had been charged with dangerous driving and the other with careless driving. For instance, there were two cases in which an old woman had been knocked down in the centre of a pedestrian crossing by a vehicle alleged to have been driven without due care; one defendant was charged with dangerous driving and the other with careless driving. There were two further cases in which the driver of a vehicle failed to stop at an Army road block and narrowly missed the soldier directing traffic; one defendant was charged with dangerous driving and the other with careless driving. These cases are a useful reminder of the problems which face the police and prosecutors when there are a number of possible charges of differing levels of seriousness but which are not obviously distinguishable, and of the need for clear policy directives if allegations of discrimination are to be avoided.

There was also some evidence from the Belfast City Commission survey to suggest that Roman Catholics were sometimes charged with more serious offences than Protestants for what appeared to be similar acts. This was most apparent in firearms cases. A person found with firearms or ammunition may be charged with a number of different offences under the Firearms Act (Northern Ireland) 1969: (i) possession with intent to endanger life or property (s.14); (ii) possession with intent to resist arrest (s.15); (iii) carrying them with criminal intent (s.16); (iv) carrying them in a public place (s.17); (v) possession in suspicious circumstances (s.19A); and (vi) possession without a certificate (s.1). These offences carry different maximum sentences, from 14 years down to 3 years imprisonment, and are regarded as more or less serious accordingly.

In the cases studied, Roman Catholics were more frequently charged with the more serious offences; for instance 119 (33%) of the 367 charges laid against those identified as Protestants were for the least serious offence of possession without a certificate, compared with only 60 (18%) of the 346 charges against Roman Catholics. (See Appendix, Table VI) This difference was even more striking in the analysis of cases reported in the *Belfast Telegraph* over the same period: two thirds of the charges reported against Roman Catholics were for the most serious offence of possession with intent to endanger life or property, compared with one third of the charges reported against Protestants; conversely one third of the charges reported against Protestants were for the least serious offence of possession without a certificate compared with only one in twenty for Roman Catholics. (See Appendix, Table VII)

It does not necessarily follow from these figures that Roman Catholics are being unjustly treated. Each case merits a more or less serious charge depending on the number of firearms involved and the circumstances in which they are found. The various charges in the Belfast City Commission survey were further analysed according to whether the arms or ammunition were found in the search of a house, in a car, on the defendant's person or otherwise. The results of this analysis are set out in Table 5.5:

Table 5.5 **Firearms charges in the Belfast City Commission survey analysed according to the circumstances in which the arms or ammunition were found.**

| *Offence* | *Search of house* *Prot.* | *Roman Cath.* | *Search of car* *Prot.* | *Roman Cath.* | *Search of person* *Prot.* | *Roman Cath.* | *Other* *Prot.* | *Roman Cath.* |
|---|---|---|---|---|---|---|---|---|
| No certificate (s.1) | 32<br>47% | 26<br>32% | 48<br>36% | 8<br>15% | 12<br>40% | 6<br>12% | 8<br>8% | 2<br>2% |
| In public place/ in suspicious circustances (ss.17 and 19) | 25<br>37% | 28<br>36% | 46<br>34% | 20<br>38% | 15<br>50% | 31<br>60% | 41<br>40% | 43<br>46% |
| To endanger life/ to resist arrest/ with criminal intent (ss. 14-16) | 11<br>16% | 26<br>32% | 41<br>30% | 25<br>47% | 3<br>10% | 15<br>29% | 54<br>52% | 48<br>52% |
| **Total** | **68**<br>**100%** | **80**<br>**100%** | **135**<br>**100%** | **53**<br>**100%** | **30**<br>**100%** | **52**<br>**100%** | **103**<br>**100%** | **93**<br>**100%** |

The most striking feature of the analysis is the difference in treatment between cases in which arms were found on the defendant's person and those where they were in a car; 40% and 36% respectively of the charges against Protestants in such cases were of the least serious offence of having no certificate, compared with 12% and 15% respectively of the charges against Roman Catholics. Given the numerous occasions on which gunmen in Belfast have carried out murderous attacks from cars or on the street it is difficult to justify this difference. The prosecuting authorities seem to have been rather more ready to accept the explanation that the guns were for defensive rather than offensive purposes from Protestants than from Roman Catholics.

#### Withdrawal and reduction of charges

One of the initial objectives of our study which it proved impossible to carry out in practice was an assessment of the practice of the courts in withdrawing or reducing charges. In the magistrates courts it was extremely difficult to gather much information on decisions of this kind in open court. It was often difficult to assess whether or not any charges had in fact been withdrawn or reduced. Only in respect of some motoring offences was the matter raised in open court, and in general no information was given of the reasons for the withdrawal or reduction.

Some more information was available in respect of the Belfast City Commission cases. A detailed analysis of the outcome of the charges against both Protestant and Roman Catholic defendants is set out in Table 5.6:

Table 5.6 **The outcome of all charges preferred against Protestants and Roman Catholics at Belfast City Commission, January - June 1973**

| | *Protestant* | | *R.Catholic* | | *Religion Unknown* | |
|---|---|---|---|---|---|---|
| | No. | % | No. | % | No. | % |
| Defendant failed to appear | 9 | 2 | 21 | 5 | 2 | 11 |
| Charge withdrawn by prosecution | 171 | 31 | 112 | 24 | 1 | 5 |
| Charge withdrawn/no verdict by direction of judge | 2 | 0 | 24 | 5 | 2 | 11 |
| Not guilty by direction of judge | 32 | 6 | 44 | 10 | 4 | 21 |
| Acquitted by jury | 81 | 15 | 28 | 6 | 3 | 16 |
| Jury disagrees/retrial | 3 | 1 | 6 | 1 | 1 | 5 |
| Convicted by jury | 256 | 46 | 226 | 49 | 6 | 32 |
| | 554 | 100 | 461 | 100 | 19 | 100 |
| Adjourned | 74 | | 129 | | 33 | |
| **Total charges** | 628 | | 590 | | 52 | |

The figures show that a rather higher proportion of charges against Protestants (31%) were withdrawn by the prosecuting authorities than against Roman Catholics (24%). On the other hand the judge ordered an acquittal or no verdict for more of the charges against Roman Catholics (15%) than Protestants (6%). It would appear from this that the prosecuting authorities have been rather more ready to withdraw charges against Protestant defendants and to press doubtful charges against Roman Catholics, but that the judges have gone some way to correct the balance. Though the net result would appear to be a rough equality of treatment, the analysis does suggest that more care should be taken by the prosecuting authorities to apply the same criteria in all cases.

**Conviction and acquittal**

There is no objective way of assessing whether a court's decision to convict or acquit an accused person is right or wrong, and thus no fully satisfactory means of investigating any possible bias on the part of magistrates or juries in this respect. However, there are three specific problems which merit some discussion: first, in respect of the magistrates courts, the problem of verdicts reached on what appears to the observer in court to be inadequate evidence; second, the practice of the security authorities of 'correcting' unsatisfactory verdicts by rearresting those acquitted in court under the Special Powers Act; and third, the problem of perverse verdicts by juries. The evidence which our studies have revealed on each is necessarily subjective, but the issues raised are nonetheless of some importance in their effect on public confidence in the courts.

The observers who took part in the magistrates court survey were asked to comment on any decision which seemed to them to merit special attention. In addition we were able to make some assessment of the various verdicts from the evidence recorded. In respect of the 'non-political' cases there was nothing to suggest that the evidence was inadequate to meet the requirement of proof beyond reasonable doubt. In a number of the 'political' cases, however, particularly those involving charges of rioting, this could not always be stated with the same degree of certainty.

In a typical riot case there are two entirely different stories as to the circumstances in which the accused was arrested, that of the soldiers or police and that of the defendant. There was a direct conflict of this kind in all but one of the cases in the sample. The magistrates in the majority of cases accepted the version given by the security forces. But in some of these it was difficult to agree that the criterion of proof beyond reasonable doubt had been met. Consider the following examples from the sample:

*Case A:* There was rioting in Derry between 2.00 p.m. and 7.00 p.m. At 4.00 p.m. a youth in white shoes was observed in the riot through binoculars by the army from an observation post. At 7.00 p.m. the defendant, who was wearing white shoes, was seen by a patrol coming down William Street. He was arrested because the patrol had been told that one of the rioters was wearing white shoes. He denied that he was in the riot and claimed he was elsewhere. He was found guilty.

*Case B:* A corporal in a patrol in the Falls Road stopped and asked the identity of the defendant. The patrol then moved on and asked the identity of another person. According to army witnesses, while he was checking this person's identity a crowd gathered about 50 yards away and started throwing stones at the patrol. It is claimed that the defendant was at the front of the crowd. No arrest was made at the time. Later the patrol came across the defendant again going in the opposite direction to the trouble. They stopped and questioned him. Then they arrested him for riotous behaviour. The defendant claimed that it was a case of mistaken identity. He had not taken part in any riot. He had gone out to buy fish and chips. When he was arrested he was standing in a doorway talking to his girlfriend. If he had been in a riot he would have run away when he saw the patrol approaching for the second time. The Magistrate agreed that it was a problem of identification. But he thought that the prosecution case rested on positive identification. The defendant was found guilty.

*Case C:* A soldier on top of some flats picked out three youths from a crowd which was rioting. They later left and as they did so the soldier lost sight of them. A minute later he saw one of them again. He was able to identify him because he was wearing a denim jacket and trousers. The soldier asked a patrol to pick him up. The defendant claimed that he was not throwing stones and that it was a case of mistaken identity. Denim jackets and trousers were common items of clothing in the area. The defendant was found guilty.

These examples show very clearly the problems which the courts have had to face during the Northern Ireland emergency. Riot cases are almost always highly emotive and politically significant. The magistrates are clearly under pressure from the security forces and from certain sections of the public to convict those brought before them to deter others from becoming involved in riotous confrontations. On the other hand to permit a conviction in doubtful circumstances, when those concerned in the area will undoubtedly know of the injustice of the case, will equally clearly decrease the level of public confidence in the courts. This sense of injustice in some riot cases may have been exacerbated by the behaviour of some soldiers in the court, who have made no attempt to conceal their pleasure at their success in obtaining a conviction. The correct balance between the desire of the courts to support the security authorities and their desire to sustain public confidence in the principle that proof must be established beyond reasonable doubt is not easy to attain. We are not satisfied that the security forces and the police have helped by their choice of cases to bring before the courts.

A similar point may be made in relation to the numerous cases in which the security authorities have made use of their powers under the Special Powers Act to rearrest persons who have been acquitted of all charges against them either by direction of the court or by a jury verdict. There were no reports of such cases in the magistrates court sample, or in the survey of higher court decisions. But there has been a continuing series of incidents of this kind since the introduction of internment without trial in August 1971. The Attorney-General has stated in reply to a Parliamentary question that since March 1972, 30 persons had been rearrested after acquittal and detained under the procedures current at that time.[16] The Attorney-General stressed in giving these figures that no person would be rearrested and detained in this way merely on the basis of the evidence of the charges which had been dismissed in court, without other evidence of involvement in terrorist activities. But even if this claim is true, the effect of such cases on public confidence in the system of justice cannot be overestimated.

It is clearly tempting for the authorities to make use of their powers to keep suspected terrorists in custody when they sincerely believe that charges against them have been dismissed on technical grounds or by a perverse verdict. The policy of relying on the ordinary courts whenever possible, however, when it is viewed in the light of these cases, looks suspiciously like a means of legitimising administrative internment. The practice should be discontinued forthwith.

**The selection of juries and perverse verdicts.**

The third item of complaint in this context is of a rather different character. It is sometimes alleged that there is an element of discrimination in the higher courts in Northern Ireland as a result of the fact that juries are predominantly Protestant and may on occasions return perverse verdicts in political cases.

In Northern Ireland householders only are eligible for jury service. This property qualification, which was removed in Britain some years ago, guarantees that a larger proportion of Protestants than Roman Catholics are called for jury service because proportionately more Protestants are householders. In addition it is sometimes alleged that juries have in the past been carefully selected in important cases by pro-Unionist court officials to ensure that a satisfactory verdict is reached. It has further been alleged that Roman Catholic representation is on occasions curtailed by the exercise of the right of the Crown to stand by as many jurors as it pleases, and thus in effect to select a jury which is all Protestant and accordingly likely to be of a Unionist persuasion. This can readily be achieved by challenging all prospective jurors who appear to be Roman Catholics either from their names or from the area in which they live. In important cases it is in fact the rule rather than the exception for the prosecutor to challenge jurors in order to exclude committed 'Republicans' and thus achieve what is considered to be a balanced jury. This procedure might not appear to be objectionable to an independent observer. But to a member of the minority community it is merely one more indication of the partiality of the judicial system as a whole. Since Crown Counsel have frequently been directly connected with the Unionist regime, the impression is reinforced that the government and the courts are not separate institutions and that the administration of justice is a political as well as a legal process.

The implication of these complaints over the composition of juries is that innocent Roman Catholic defendants may have been convicted and guilty Protestants acquitted. There was a good deal of disquiet on this score following the acquittal of five Protestants charged with blowing up water pipelines outside Belfast in the early stages of the current emergency. More recently, with the increase of terrorist activities on the Loyalist side, there have been renewed allegations of perverse verdicts. During the second reading of the Emergency Powers (Northern Ireland) Bill the Attorney-General referred to a number of cases in a recent assize at Armagh in which the verdicts in cases involving Loyalists appeared to his informants to be contrary to the evidence.[17] In one instance a man found in a car with a gun was acquitted of unlawful possession of firearms; in another three men who were seen to throw a gun from a car being pursued by an Army patrol were also acquitted; in a third case involving the hijacking of a lorry, the cargo was found in a UDA club and the documents were in the handwriting of the accused, but the verdict was again an acquittal; in the fourth the leader of a UDA unit who had been identified as having taken part in an armed robbery of a Post Office was acquitted. Since the Attorney-General's speech there have been a number of similar allegations in respect of cases heard in Belfast.

The findings of the survey of Belfast City Commission cases, set out in Table 5.6 above, bear out suspicions on the partiality or perhaps intimidation of Belfast juries. Though the figures for convictions in charges against Protestants and Roman Catholics were roughly equal, the rate of jury acquittal for charges against Protestants (15%) was more than double the rate of jury acquittal for charges against Roman Catholics (6%). As in the case of the withdrawal of charges, however, the judges appear to have gone some way to correct the balance by directing a not guilty verdict in 10% of the charges against Roman Catholics compared with only 6% of those against Protestants.

It would be wrong to draw any firm conclusion from these findings. It may be that some jurors have been politically biased. It may be that some have been intimidated. Or it may be that they have honestly believed that the prosecution has not proved its case beyond reasonable doubt. But there can be little doubt that the confidence of the minority community in the impartiality of the courts has been shaken by a number of widely publicised cases of allegedly perverse acquittals of charges against Protestants. It is significant in this context that our initial survey of cases reported in the *Belfast Telegraph*, set out in Table VIII of the Appendix, showed an even higher acquittal rate of 35% for charges against those identified as Protestants compared with only 11% for those identified as Roman Catholics. But even if this degree of selective reporting is allowed for, it would seem that the real difference in acquittal rates is sufficient to justify the temporary suspension of jury trial for terrorist offences as provided in the Northern Ireland (Emergency Provisions) Act 1973. Arguments as to the desirability of maintaining jury trial even in emergency conditions which may seem convincing to an English audience are less compelling in a divided community like Northern Ireland. To restore public confidence in jury verdicts it would be necessary to ensure that juries in politically sensitive cases were broadly representative of both communities. But this would be difficult to achieve without making radical changes in the law on jury selection and challenge. A provision for the trial of terrorist or political offences before a bench of judges or a judge assisted by representative assessors would seem to be the best alternative in a difficult situation.

**Sentencing**

The main allegation on sentencing in Magistrates Courts and to a lesser extent in higher courts has been that Roman Catholics have been given more severe sentences than Protestants for similar offences.

It was not possible to make any valid assessment of this allegation in respect of the 'political' cases covered in our Magistrates Courts survey since so few resulted in a conviction, and most of those which did received a mandatory sentence. In respect of the 'non-political' cases, however, it was possible to make some assessment. For motoring offences, among which there were large numbers of similar cases, a comparison of maximum, minimum and average sentences revealed a high level of consistency in sentencing. Though the religion of the defendant was not always revealed, there was no evidence to suggest discrimination of any kind. There was likewise no evidence to suggest sectarian bias in respect of other 'ordinary' offences. There was some evidence of class bias, however, in respect of ordinary property offences. The four middle class defendants who appeared on charges of this kind appeared to receive lighter sentences than working class defendants charged with similar offences. For instance, in one case an 18-year old middle class defendant stole £20; he was fined £10 and ordered to pay restitution. In another case a middle class defendant was found guilty of stealing £49; he was given a conditional discharge. In contrast, a labourer charged with theft of property costing 58p was fined £15. None of these defendants had any previous convictions.

The analysis of sentences in the Belfast City Commission cases also indicated that the judges were generally fairly consistent in dealing with offences of the same type. In respect of firearms cases, however, there was a small difference in the treatment of charges against Protestants and Roman Catholics. The figures for average sentences, set out in Table 5.7, show that Roman Catholics received a heavier average sentence on charges of carrying arms in public or with criminal intent and of possessing firearms or ammunition in suspicious circumstances.

Table 5.7 **Average sentences imposed for firearms charges against Protestants and Roman Catholics, Belfast City Commission January-June 1973.**

| | *Protestant* | *Roman Catholic* |
|---|---|---|
| No certificate for firearms | 9 months | 12 months |
| No certificate for ammunition | 11 months | 11 months |
| Firearms/ammunition in suspicious circumstances | 2.3 years | 3.3 years |
| Carrying firearms in a public place | 2.3 years | 3.4 years |
| Carrying firearms with criminal intent | 4.2 years | 6.3 years |
| Possession of firearms/ammunition to endanger life | 6.4 years | 6.8 years |

There are many possible explanations for differences in the length of sentences imposed for apparently similar offences. The judge may regard the incidents out of which the charges arise as more or less serious. The previous record of the defendant may be crucial to the final decision. In addition, individual judges will have different general attitudes to the seriousness of offences and to the objectives of punishment. They will perceive and categorise the information which is given to them in different ways. Their decisions will be influenced by their social class, personality, political affiliation and social attitudes. It would be highly dangerous, therefore, to conclude that the variations in sentences revealed in our surveys were always due to sectarian bias.

On the other hand it is clearly of the greatest importance that the sentences imposed on Protestants and Roman Catholics in Northern Ireland should be patently fair in all the circumstances, and that they should be seen to be fair. Even if the differences in sentence between Protestants and Roman Catholic defendants which have been noted were objectively justified, for example, on the basis of the gravity of the incidents involved or the previous record of the accused, this did not appear from the press reports of the cases upon which public attitudes are largely based. This would suggest that much more attention should be paid by judges to making explicit in open court the reasons for their decision to impose a given sentence, and in particular the reasons for any variation from the norm for offences of a given kind.

It does not follow, of course, that everyone will immediately recognise the justice of the reasons given for differentiation. There are people in Northern Ireland who do not wish to be persuaded of the impartiality of the judicial system, and who will always be ready to make selective comparisons of cases which appear to demonstrate a bias one way or the other. Two cases compared in a press statement issued by the Association for Legal Justice illustrate this point. A contrast was made between the case of Mr. Cosgrove, who received a three year prison sentence for having a list of police car numbers in his possession (see above p. 43), and the case of a Protestant who received a suspended sentence on a charge of malicious wounding following the death of a Mr. McFarlane:

> In the case of the death of a Mr. McFarlane in September 1972 the Public Prosecutions Office entered a *nolle prosequi* on an indictment of manslaughter, reduced from murder even after the impannelling of a jury to hear the case on 22 February 1973. As a consequence, judicial cognisance of a death consequent on violence was precluded. A sentence of twelve months imprisonment was imposed on the Loyalist gang member held responsible on a charge of malicious wounding. There is a striking contrast with the vicious pursuit of an excessive penalty in the case of Peter Cosgrove, a Coleraine student where no implication of violence or subversion was sustained.[18]

It might be assumed that this was a case of death from Loyalist aggression, and thus of sectarian bias in the reduction of the charge. Further investigation revealed that Mr. McFarlane's death was caused by his hitting his head on a stone floor after falling during a pub brawl. Though the deceased was a Roman Catholic and the defendant a Protestant there was apparently no sectarian implication. This process of selective comparison is very common in Northern Ireland, and is likely to continue to prove effective as long as members of the public lack general confidence in the administration of justice.

One final aspect of the sentencing process must be mentioned. Under the Criminal Justice (Temporary Provisions) Act (Northern Ireland) magistrates were required to impose mandatory sentences in certain cases.[19] There was some evidence from our study of the operation of the magistrates courts that this requirement has an adverse effect on public attitudes to the courts. Many members of the public were reported to have been dissatisfied with the mandatory sentences imposed in certain cases. In some cases the magistrates themselves were also unhappy. In one case the magistrate remarked that the compulsory sentence was too high but that it had to be imposed. In another the magistrate remarked that it was with the greatest reluctance that he imposed the mandatory six month sentence. There were other cases in which though no comment was made the mandatory sentence was clearly inappropriate. In one case a Protestant youth of 20, who had been taken to the police station when his father found him with a single round of ammunition, was given a mandatory six month sentence. In another a Roman Catholic was convicted of having possession of an empty shotgun cartridge and was likewise given a mandatory sentence of six months. Cases such as these show the difficulties which may be caused by any attempt to impose uniformity on the courts by legislation.

**Conclusion**

It would be wrong to draw any firm conclusion from the material in this chapter on the question of discrimination or bias on the part of the judiciary in Northern Ireland. The survey made of decision-making in the magistrates' courts and higher courts has not been comprehensive, and we have not had full access to all the information which might properly affect decisions on the selection of charges, the granting of bail, conviction or acquittal, and sentence. A researcher in this sphere would ideally like to be present at, or at least informed of, all the stages in the decision making process and to have access to all the material available to the decison-makers, whether the police, the prosecuting authorities, counsel and the court before passing his own judgement on the merits of any particular decision or on the existence or absence of conscious or unconscious bias. At the best of times, this information would be difficult to obtain and the analysis would be very time-consuming. When, as in Northern Ireland, there are genuine problems over security, to add to the standard offical attitude on the confidentiality of pre-trial proceedings, the likelihood of anyone being permitted to carry out a fully satisfactory research study is still further reduced.

Nonetheless the surveys which we have been able to make of the working of the courts under the present emergency conditions in Northern Ireland, with all the imperfections which have been referred to, do suggest that there is a small but cumulative measure of (perhaps unconscious) sympathy with Protestants and Loyalists. This applies particularly to the decision to prosecute and the selection or withdrawal of charges by the police and the prosecuting authorities. It also applies to some jury verdicts. The judges themselves appear to have gone some way to correct these prior inequalities through their power to direct acquittals but there was some evidence of inequality in sentences for firearms offences.

There is no clear evidence as to the reason for this bias, insofar as it does exist, but it seems likely that it is due to the feeling among the police and the courts that the initiative in the continuing civil disorders and guerrilla warfare has been on the Republican side, and that Loyalist offences have been committed in response to, or in reaction to Republican aggression and provocation. This interpretation would not be shared by members of the minority community, who would probably take the view that the present round of sectarian conflict was sparked off by Protestant aggression in the early civil rights phase, and that the resort to terrorist tactics was also first made by Protestants. This would go some way to explain the difference in treatment of firearms offences, which form the basis of many of the observed differences in the treatment of members of the two communities.

There is a good deal less doubt that the extent of bias in the courts in the eyes of the minority community has been greatly amplified by a process of selective reporting. It is relatively easy, as the surveys we have made show, to select from the range of cases dealt with in the courts a few individual comparisons in which a Republican has been much more harshly treated than a Loyalist in respect of what appear on the surface to be similar cases. Similar selective comparisons have also been made by Loyalists. The widespread and continued reporting of such adverse comparisons has fostered the view among Roman Catholics and to a lesser extent among Protestants that the whole system of courts is structurally biased against them and in favour of the other side. On the basis of our surveys we do not think that such a judgment would be justified. The large majority of cases appeared to be dealt with fairly and without discrimination of any kind. But the minority of cases in which there is a real difference of treatment affect public attitudes to the courts and to the system of justice as a whole to an extent out of all proportion to their number.

If this assessment is accurate, two comments are appropriate. First, the prosecuting authorities and the judiciary must realise that every decision they make will be used in selective reporting if it varies in any degree from the current norm. This might be avoided by a more open and direct admission by the prosecuting authorities and the courts of the need to preserve complete equality of treatment. This would involve a much closer watch on the treatment of such cases than is apparently now kept, and a willingness to make the results publicly available.

The second point is that insofar as differences in treatment are justified by the special circumstances of a particular case, such as the previous record of an accused person, it is essential that these circumstances be made public. All judicial decisions should be made on a reasoned basis and the reasons for an apparent difference in treatment from the norm made explicit. This applies as much to the process of the selection of charges as to the question of bail and sentencing.

Both these points are directly related to the more general issue of the maintenance of public confidence in the impartiality of the courts. Despite the constant assertions which are made by the authorities, we believe that there is a widespread lack of public confidence among the minority community in the absolute impartiality of the judicial system. Until the importance of this is accepted by the courts and the security authorities, the steps which are necessary to counteract it cannot be taken. We also believe that taking these steps, such as maintaining an open system of comparison of the treatment of members of the two communities and giving explicit reasons for judicial decision in general, would help to eliminate what element of unconscious bias there is in the system.

**References**


1. 855 H.C. Deb., col. 278, 17 April 1973.
2. *Irish Times,* 2 December 1969.
3. *Commentary upon the White Paper (Command Paper 558) entitled 'A Record of Constructive Change',* Belfast 1971.
4. November 1972.
5. The sentence was reduced to a fine on appeal.
6. *Belfast Telegraph,* 8 January 1973.
7. *Belfast Telegraph,* 10 January 1973.
8. *Report of the Advisory Committee on Police in Northern Ireland,* Cmd. 535, Belfast 1969, para. 142.
9. Report of the Working Party on Public Prosecutions, Cmd. 554, Belfast 1972.
10. Further research in this area is currently under consideration.
11. *Bail or Custody* by Michael King and Christine Jackson, 1971.
12. 855 H.C. Deb., col. 386, 17 April 1973.
13. Provisions of this kind have been included in the Northern Ireland (Emergency Provisions) Act 1973.
14. 'Legal Aid for Summary Trials in Northern Ireland' by D. Greer, *Northern Ireland Legal Quarterly,* Vol. 22, 1971, p. 431.
15. Parliamentary answer, 3 August 1972.
16. H.C. Deb, Standing Committee B, col. 77, 8 May 1973.
17. 855 H.C. Deb., cols. 381-2, 17 April 1973.
18. *Irish Times,* 2 March 1973.
19. See generally 'The "Minimum Sentences" Act' by Kevin Boyle, *Northern Ireland Legal Quarterly,* Vol. 21, 1970, p. 425. The Act was repealed in August 1973 by the Northern Ireland (Emergency Provisions) Act.

# Conclusion

The initial objective of this study was to assess the validity of the allegations which have been made about the administration of justice in Northern Ireland, and to determine what degree of justification there might be for the widespread lack of confidence in the judicial system among members of the Roman Catholic community. It must be remembered, however, that the material available to us does not justify more than tentative findings and that our conclusions must accordingly be treated with some caution.

It must also be remembered that we have based our research on an acceptance of certain facts about judicial systems in general. In any state the judges are appointed to uphold the existing constitution. In addition in any western democracy the judicial system may be expected to uphold the status quo in class structure and in the distribution of property. It is legitimate to argue that this is an unsatisfactory state of affairs. We have not considered this wider issue. We have only been concerned with the question of whether the judicial system in Northern Ireland has discriminated between Protestants and Roman Catholics in the application of the law.

It is clear to us that the judicial system in Northern Ireland has never enjoyed the respect and confidence of the minority community. One indication of this was the fact that at no time during the civil rights campaign of the late 1960s was any case raised in the courts which required the judges to determine any of the many allegations of discrimination against Roman Catholics at the local government level. Some attempts were made to initiate proceedings but the problems of procedure and finance were never surmounted, and when an application for legal aid was turned down the attempt was abandoned. When an issue was eventually raised in the courts in 1968 over the interpretation of the Special Powers Act the reluctance of the majority of the judges both in the Northern Ireland Court of Appeal and in the British House of Lords to interfere in executive decisions resulted in the rejection of the case. The result in these cases reinforced the initial lack of confidence among the minority in the judicial system. The failure of the civil rights leaders to pursue or obtain a legal remedy is in our view to be attributed to two major factors. First there was the pre-existing lack of confidence in the prospects of winning any case in the courts. This was due largely to the fact that so many judicial appointments had been made from those who openly supported the Unionist regime. Second there was the unsatisfactory performance of the legal system in response to those issues which were raised. Neither the lawyers nor the judges in Northern Ireland had been trained to deal directly with the broad issues of social and legal justice raised in the civil rights campaign. The current

British tradition of relying on highly precise and technical points of procedure and of erring on the side of caution in apportioning blame was highly inappropriate. This would seem to us to be a compelling argument for the enactment of a strong Bill of Rights for Northern Ireland.

In respect of this stage of the civil rights campaign in Northern Ireland we have no reason to suppose that the response of the Northern Ireland judiciary was any different from that which might have been expected in any other British jurisdiction.

In the surveys we conducted in 1972 and 1973 we distinguished between political and non-political offences. We found that no discrimination was involved in the treatment of non-political offences, but that there is some justification for allegations of discrimination in dealing with political offences. The evidence for this is clearest at the pre-trial stage. Different standards would appear to have been applied as between Roman Catholic and Protestant defendants in the selection of charges, especially in firearms cases, and in the advice given to courts on the granting of bail. At the trial stage, there would appear to be a greater readiness on the part of juries to convict Roman Catholic defendants and to acquit Protestant defendants of 'terrorist' offences. There have also been some differences in levels of sentencing. It is not clear whether these are to be attributed to the different facts of the various cases, to the previous records of the defendants, to the idiosyncracies of judges and magistrates or to some element of conscious or unconscious discrimination.

Since the introduction of internment without trial in August 1971 the Northern Ireland judges have taken a more direct approach to their responsibilities as guarantors of justice and civil liberties. But this welcome trend has been effectively cancelled out by the super-imposition of 'executive justice' on the decisions of the courts. The numerous cases in which the security forces have used their powers under the Special Powers Act to rearrest persons acquitted or ordered to be released by the courts, and the failure to pursue cases arising out of alleged misconduct by members of the security forces with the same vigour as those against suspected terrorists, have been extremely potent factors in the continuing lack of confidence among the minority community in the judicial system as a whole.

The impact of all these factors has undoubtedly been amplified by a process of selective reporting by those whose objective it has been to discredit the institutions of a state whose legitimacy they reject. Nonetheless there has been in our view sufficient cause for complaint over the ineffectiveness of judicial guarantees against discrimination, over bias in the enforcement of the criminal law in terrorist offences, and over the superimposition of 'executive justice' on court decisions to nullify the continual appeals by both Ulster and British politicians for trust in the judicial system.

On a wider level of analysis it seems to us that the lack of confidence among Roman Catholics in the judicial system as a whole, whether justified or not, has been a major factor in the continuing crisis in Northern Ireland. This is not to say that confidence in a completely impartial judiciary would have been an answer to the structural discrimination which has been built up in Northern Ireland over a long period of time, or to the process of escalation in the communal confrontations and disorders which developed. But it seems likely to us that a greater commitment on the part of the government to eradicating any differential treatment of Protestants and Roman Catholics in the enforcement of the law and to ensuring that complaints against the security forces were fully investigated and dealt with would have helped to halt the trend towards violence. What happened instead was that the judicial system was openly used by the government, both before and after the imposition of direct rule from Westminster, as a buttress to the existing order. The Unionist government reacted repressively when its authority was called in question, and sought to suppress any criticism or complaint raised against it. The Westminster government reacted similarly to allegations over misconduct by the security forces. Both resorted to the appointment of judicial enquiries to report on issues which could and should have been dealt with directly in the courts. Both showed utter contempt for the rule of law.

This study makes clear the consequences of such a course of action. First on a moral and political level it is dangerous to attempt to combine continued proclamations about the independence of the judiciary and the law with progressive interference with that independence. Second and more practically interference with the rule of law is likely to be positively counter-productive. This is especially the case where there are identifiable and self-identifying groups who see themselves threatened or oppressed by derogations from the rule of law. The case of Northern Ireland with its deep and clear-cut communal division is an extreme example of this. Public confidence in the institutions of law and justice is bound up with a popular conception of the rule of law. If reliance on the independence and impartiality of the judges is to play a part in achieving a just settlement to the present crisis, much more attention will have to be paid by all concerned to the crucial issue of restoring social confidence in the administration of justice.

# Appendix

**TABLE I: Number and proportion of cases observed and their outcome**

**Magistrates Courts Survey 1972**

| | | *Total No. of cases observed* | *No. of Bail/remand Decisions* | *No. of Convic-tions* | *No. of Dismis-sals* |
|---|---|---|---|---|---|
| **A.** | **Political:** | | | | |
| 1. | Rioting | 15 | 1 | 12 | 2 |
| 2. | Firearms | 56 | 51 | 5 | – |
| 3. | Explosives | 11 | 11 | – | – |
| 4. | Against the person | 15 | 10 | 5 | – |
| 5. | Other | 22 | 1 | 21 | – |
| **B.** | **Motoring:** | | | | |
| 1. | Quality of driving | 79 | – | 72 | 7 |
| 2. | State while driving | 51 | – | 51 | – |
| 3. | State of vehicle | 14 | – | 14 | – |
| 4. | Parking | 15 | – | 14 | 1 |
| 5. | Paper work | 39 | – | 39 | – |
| **C.** | **Property:** | | | | |
| 1. | Shoplifting | 25 | – | 25 | – |
| 2. | Burglary | 25 | 4 | 21 | – |
| 3. | Other theft | 51 | 5 | 45 | 1 |
| 4. | Fraud | 29 | 2 | 27 | – |
| **D.** | **Miscellaneous:** | | | | |
| 1. | Against the person | 35 | 5 | 30 | – |
| 2. | Disorderly behaviour | 43 | – | 39 | 4 |
| 3. | Other specified | 23 | 4 | 19 | – |
| 4. | Other unspecified | 20 | 20 | – | – |
| | **Total** | **568** | **114** | **439** | **15** |

**TABLE II: Number and proportion of cases observed in each court**

**Magistrates Courts Survey 1972**

| *Offence Group* | *Total No. of offences observed* No. | % | *Belfast Custody* No. | % | *Belfast Summons* No. | % | *Coleraine* No. | % | *Limavady* No. | % |
|---|---|---|---|---|---|---|---|---|---|---|
| 1. Political | 119 | 20.9 | 104 | 33.8 | — | — | 1 | 2.5 | 3 | 13.6 |
| 2. Motoring | 198 | 34.8 | 18 | 5.8 | 77 | 98.7 | 22 | 55.0 | 12 | 54.5 |
| 3. Property | 130 | 22.9 | 93 | 30.2 | — | 1.3 | 13 | 32.5 | 4 | 18.2 |
| 4. Miscellaneous | 121 | 21.3 | 93 | 30.2 | 1 | — | 4 | 10.0 | 3 | 13.6 |
| **Total** | **568** | **100.0** | **308** | **100.0** | **78** | **100.0** | **40** | **100.0** | **22** | **100.0** |

| *Offence* | *L'derry* No. | % | *Lisburn* No. | % | *Lurgan* No. | % | *Portadown* No. | % | *Newtownbreda* No. | % |
|---|---|---|---|---|---|---|---|---|---|---|
| 1. Political | 5 | 27.8 | 4 | 14.3 | — | — | 2 | 8.3 | — | — |
| 2. Motoring | 8 | 44.4 | 12 | 42.8 | 22 | 57.9 | 16 | 66.7 | 11 | 91.6 |
| 3. Property | 5 | 27.8 | 7 | 25.0 | 5 | 13,2 | 2 | 8.3 | 1 | 8.4 |
| 4. Miscellaneous | — | — | 5 | 17.9 | 11 | 28.9 | 4 | 16.7 | — | |
| **Total** | **18** | **100.0** | **28** | **100.0** | **38** | **100.0** | **24** | **100.0** | **12** | **100.0** |

**Table III: Number and proportion of persons convicted or dismissed for each of the four categories of offence.**

**Magistrates Courts Survey 1972**

| | *Guilty* | | *Not Guilty* | | *Total* | |
|---|---|---|---|---|---|---|
| Political | 19 | 42.3 | 26 | 57.7 | 45 | 100 |
| Motoring | 145 | 73.2 | 53 | 26.8 | 198 | 100 |
| Property | 101 | 84.9 | 18 | 15.1 | 119 | 100 |
| Miscellaneous | 66 | 71.7 | 26 | 28.3 | 92 | 100 |
| **Total:** | **331** | **72.9** | **123** | **27.1** | **454** | **100** |

**Table IV: Number of defendants legally represented shown by offence category**

**Magistrates Courts Survey 1972**

| | *Legally Represented* | | *Not Legally Represented* | | *Total* | |
|---|---|---|---|---|---|---|
| **A. Political** | *No.* | *%* | *No.* | *%* | *No.* | *%* |
| 1. Rioting | 13 | 86.7 | 2 | 13.3 | 15 | 100 |
| 2. Firearms | 40 | 65.6 | 21 | 34.4 | 61 | 100 |
| 3. Explosives | 6 | 100 | – | – | 6 | 100 |
| 4. Against the person | 9 | 60 | 6 | 40 | 15 | 100 |
| 5. Other | 14 | 63.6 | 8 | 36.4 | 22 | 100 |
| **B. Motoring** | | | | | | |
| 1. Quality of driving | 60 | 75.9 | 19 | 24.1 | 79 | 100 |
| 2. State while driving | 36 | 70.6 | 15 | 29.4 | 51 | 100 |
| 3. State of vehicle | 5 | 35.7 | 9 | 64.3 | 14 | 100 |
| 4. Parking | – | – | 15 | 100 | 15 | 100 |
| 5. Paper work | 9 | 23.1 | 30 | 76.9 | 39 | 100 |
| **C. Property** | | | | | | |
| 1. Shoplifting | 17 | 68.0 | 8 | 32.0 | 25 | 100 |
| 2. Burglary | 23 | 92.0 | 2 | 8.0 | 25 | 100 |
| 3. Other theft | 42 | 82.4 | 9 | 17.6 | 51 | 100 |
| 4. Fraud | 15 | 51.7 | 14 | 48.3 | 29 | 100 |
| **D. Miscellaneous** | | | | | | |
| 1. Against the person | 31 | 88.6 | 4 | 11.4 | 35 | 100 |
| 2. Disorderly behaviour | 33 | 76.7 | 10 | 23.3 | 43 | 100 |
| 3. Other specified | 16 | 69.6 | 7 | 30.4 | 23 | 100 |
| 4. Other Unspecified | 9 | 45.0 | 11 | 55.0 | 20 | 100 |
| **Total** | **378** | | **190** | | **568** | |

**Table V: Number of applications for legal aid and number of refusals of legal aid in respect of criminal proceedings in courts of summary jurisdiction in Northern Ireland.**

| CRIMINAL PROCEEDINGS | | |
|---|---|---|
| *Period* | *Number of applications* | *Number of refusals* |
| 1st April 1968 to 31st March 1969 | 1,345 | 52 |
| 1st April 1969 to 31st March 1970 | 2,519 | 100 |
| 1st April 1970 to 31st March 1971 | 4,419 | 110 |
| 1st April 1971 to 31st March 1972 | 5,395 | 187 |

**Source:** House of Commons – 3rd August, 1972.

**Table VI: Details of charges against Protestant and Roman Catholic defendants, Belfast City Commission January - June 1973**

| *Offences* | *Protestant* | *Roman Catholic* | *Religion Unknown* | *Total* |
|---|---|---|---|---|
| Murder | 10 | 5 | – | 15 |
| Attempted Murder | 16 | 10 | 1 | 27 |
| Offences against the Person | 20 | 14 | – | 34 |
| Explosive Substances Act | 9 | 85 | 2 | 96 |
| Firearms without certificates | 119 | 60 | 13 | 192 |
| Other firearms offences (ss. 4, 15, 16, 17, 19) | 171 | 187 | 18 | 376 |
| Firearms Act (s. 14) | 77 | 99 | 10 | 186 |
| Robbery | 41 | 41 | 1 | 83 |
| Other property offences (Theft Act) | 85 | 11 | 5 | 101 |
| Malicious Damage | 2 | 6 | 2 | 10 |
| Membership of unlawful association, etc. | 2 | 30 | – | 32 |
| Road Traffic Act Offences | 38 | 30 | – | 68 |
| Public Order | 23 | – | – | 23 |
| Other | 15 | 18 | – | 33 |
| **Total** | **628** | **596** | **52** | **1276** |

**Table VII The number and proportion of Roman Catholics and Protestants charged with different types of firearms offences in cases on indictment reported in the *Belfast Telegraph* between January and May 1973**

| *Charge* | *Roman Catholic* | | *Protestant* | | *Unknown* | |
|---|---|---|---|---|---|---|
| | No | % | No | % | No | % |
| Possession of firearms with intent to endanger life | 61 | 64 | 31 | 34 | 9 | 39 |
| Possession of firearms under suspicious circumstances | 21 | 22 | 30 | 33 | 9 | 39 |
| Carrying firearms in a public place | 8 | 9 | – | – | – | – |
| Possession of firearms without a certificate | 5 | 5 | 31 | 34 | 5 | 22 |
| **Total** | **95** | **100** | **92** | **100** | **23** | **100** |

**Table VIII The number and proportion of charges against convictions and acquittals in Catholics and Protestants in cases on indictment reported in the *Belfast Telegraph* between January and May 1973.**

| | *Roman Catholic* | | *Protestant* | | *Unknown* | | *Total* | |
|---|---|---|---|---|---|---|---|---|
| | No | % | No | % | No | % | No | % |
| Convictions | 257 | 89 | 111 | 65 | 38 | 73 | 406 | 79 |
| Acquittals | 32 | 11 | 61 | 35 | 16 | 27 | 109 | 21 |
| **Total** | **289** | **100** | **172** | **100** | **54** | **100** | **515** | **100** |

# The Cobden Trust

The formation of the Cobden Trust in 1963 stemmed directly from the work of the National Council for Civil Liberties (NCCL). The two work in close co-operation and their aim are the same: the protection and extension of civil liberties in Britain.

But whilst the NCCL is a voluntary organisation that takes up issues and individual cases of injustice, the Cobden Trust is a registered charity undertaking research into education work, creating a deeper understanding of civil liberties. The Trust's earlier work included research for the NCCL in connection with its publications on the rights of citizens.

The future programme of the Trust includes research into prisoners' rights, representation before administrative tribunals, the implications for civil rights of Britain's membership of the European Economic Community, the law of conspiracy and the law with regard to squatting.

**Finance**

*The Cobden Trust relies solely on public financial support: grants from Trusts covenants and donations from business firms and individuals. £10,000 is required to finance current and proposed research, to build up a Civil Liberties Research Library and to meet administrative costs. If you can help this work, you are invited to do so by completing the appropriate form and sending it to the Secretary of the Cobden Trust.*

**Covenants**

*The most effective form of help is a donation in the form of a seven-year Covenant. A covenant increases the value of your gift because the Cobden Trust can recover tax from the Inland Revenue on every £ covenanted.*

**Donations**

*Gifts to the Trust, do not have to be covenanted. Ordinary donations are also welcome and helpful in furthering the Trust's work.*

## DEED OF COVENANT: COBDEN TRUST 186 Kings Cross Road, London

NAME IN FULL I ....................................................(Mr/Mrs/Miss).

ADDRESS of ....................................................................
hereby covenant with the Trustees of the Cobden Trust that for a period of seven years, from the date hereof or during my life, whichever period shall be shorter, I will pay to the

Trustees, on the ..................... in each year, such sum as will ............. after deduction of income tax at the current rate leave in the hands of the Cobden Trust the

net sum of ..................... such sum being paid from my general fund of taxed income so that I shall receive no personal or private benefit in any of the said years from the said annual payments or any part thereof.
In witness whereof I have hereunto set my hand and seal this day of

........................................ 19 .......

Signed, Sealed and Delivered by the above named ..............................

In the presence of witness ................................................

Address ..........................................................................

Occupation .......................................................................

## BANKER'S ORDER: COBDEN TRUST

The Manager ......................................................................
(name and address of Bank)

Please pay to the credit of the CHARITIES AID FUND of the NATIONAL COUNCIL OF SOCIAL SERVICE (D) A/C No. 880043 at the National Westminster Bank Ltd., Bloomsbury Parr's Branch, 126 High Holborn, London WC1 (60.30.60) for the later credit of the COBDEN TRUST on the ........... day of ................... 19 . . . the

sum of £ ............. and the same sum on the same date each year until 19. . . .

and debit my account number accordingly.
(Office use only)

(When making each payment please quote 08107(05)

Name ...................... (Mr/Mrs/Miss)

Address ..............................

..............................

Signature .............................. Date ...................

## DONATION: COBDEN TRUST

I enclose £ .................. as a donation to the general work of the Cobden Trust.

Name ..................................................................

Address ..................................................................

..........................................................................

Date ..................................................................

Please send the completed forms to: The Secretary, The Cobden Trust, 186 Kings Cross Road, London WC1X 9DE Telephone 01-278 4575